Race and Society

The Essentials

I would like to dedicate this book to the memory of Representative John Lewis (1940–2020). May his lifetime of racial justice activism be an inspiration to us all and may his words remain in the forefront of our minds:

"When you see something that is not right, not fair, not just, you have to speak up. You have to say something, you have to do something."

Sara Miller McCune founded SAGE Publishing in 1965 to support the dissemination of usable knowledge and educate a global community. SAGE publishes more than 1000 journals and over 600 new books each year, spanning a wide range of subject areas. Our growing selection of library products includes archives, data, case studies and video. SAGE remains majority owned by our founder and after her lifetime will become owned by a charitable trust that secures the company's continued independence.

Los Angeles | London | New Delhi | Singapore | Washington DC | Melbourne

Race and Society

The Essentials

Kathleen J. Fitzgerald

The University of North Carolina at Chapel Hill

Los Angeles | London | New Delhi
Singapore | Washington DC | Melbourne

FOR INFORMATION:

SAGE Publications, Inc.
2455 Teller Road
Thousand Oaks, California 91320
E-mail: order@sagepub.com

SAGE Publications Ltd.
1 Oliver's Yard
55 City Road
London EC1Y 1SP
United Kingdom

SAGE Publications India Pvt. Ltd.
B 1/I 1 Mohan Cooperative Industrial Area
Mathura Road, New Delhi 110 044
India

SAGE Publications Asia-Pacific Pte. Ltd.
18 Cross Street #10-10/11/12
China Square Central
Singapore 048423

Acquisitions Editor: Jeff Lasser
Editorial Assistant: Tiara Beatty
Production Editor: Rebecca Lee
Copy Editor: Jared Leighton
Typesetter: C&M Digitals (P) Ltd.
Proofreader: Scott Oney
Indexer: Integra
Cover Designer: Janet Kiesel
Marketing Manager: Jennifer Jones

Printed in the United States of America

Library of Congress Cataloging-in-Publication Data

ISBN 978-1-5443-7414-7

This book is printed on acid-free paper.

20 21 22 23 24 10 9 8 7 6 5 4 3 2 1

Contents

··

Preface

••

I have been teaching the sociology of race/ethnicity for 28 years. Over those years, whenever I met someone new and shared what I did for a living, they inevitably commented on the significance of the subject at that particular historical moment—a police shooting of an unarmed person of color making headlines, the election of the nation's first Black president, the discovery of scandalous college yearbook photos of elected officials wearing blackface, professional athletes making headlines for taking a knee to protest police brutality, and so on. There was always a topical story that seemed to make that moment *the* moment for teaching and talking about race. I always laughed and said that had been true my entire career. Indeed, race, racism, and privilege are defining features of U.S. society. However, I do believe there is something unique about *this* particular historical moment, the summer of 2020. For the first time in decades, we have sustained, mass, global protests against police brutality, voluntary (and involuntary) removals of Confederate monuments, corporations retiring racist images, a discussion of reparations in the U.S. House of Representatives, and a profound desire to learn more about race and racism, if the *New York Times* best-selling nonfiction book list is any indication.

This small book is designed as an overview of the key terms and concepts and foundational research in the sociology of race/ethnicity: Race, ethnicity, racial status hierarchies, White privilege, intersectionality, assimilation, racialization, racism, prejudice, institutional racism, global White supremacy, and many more topics are introduced. We also discuss interracial intimacies, including interracial relationships; multiracial families; and biracial/multiracial identities. We conclude with a global look at race, racism, White supremacy, and efforts to heal from racial conflicts, including reconciliation projects, restorative justice, and reparations. Each chapter concludes with a section titled "Toward a More Racially Just Society," in order to help students move from talking about race and racism to combating it. Sociological topics are introduced through a topical lens and written in an accessible language for upper-level undergraduates or as a supplement to a graduate-level sociology of race/ethnicity course. It is designed to provide a foundation for giving students a language so they can have productive and necessary discussions about race, racism, and privilege and understand how to move from talk to action—how to move toward a more racially just society.

Acknowledgments

So many people contributed to this book, some in obvious ways and others in less obvious ways. In this case, the literal idea for the book came from my editor at SAGE, Jeff Lasser. I had worked with Jeff on the first edition of my coauthored text, *Sociology of Sexualities*. While we shared a glass of wine in celebration of the publication of *SOS* in New Orleans at the 2018 Southern Sociological Society Annual Meetings, he encouraged me to write a small race text, a book that covered the basic terms and concepts in the field. I wasn't immediately sold on the idea, but he planted a seed, and I warmed to the idea and eventually wrote a prospectus. Jeff is a consummate professional and an unwavering presence in a publishing world known more for constant change and upheaval than consistency. Thanks, Jeff, not just for the idea but for trusting me with it and for randomly cold-calling me during the summer of 2020 to make sure things were moving along (*Who does that?*)! I also wish to extend my gratitude to the entire team of professionals at SAGE for bringing this book to life. This is a better book because of you.

I want to thank my many students who have challenged and enlightened me over the years. I say this all the time, but it bears repeating: It is an honor and a privilege to teach college students; to bear witness to and sometimes be a catalyst for a person's intellectual growth and development during such a pivotal time in their lives is a gift I never take for granted. I was especially pleased to hear from a couple dozen former students (some from decades ago!) during the racial justice uprisings that happened across the globe in the spring and summer of 2020 to protest the police killing of George Floyd in Minneapolis, Minnesota. To know that the course you took with me was on your mind and that you wanted to learn more and do more in the face of racial injustice was profoundly humbling and inspiring. Thank you for reaching out.

To my colleagues in the Department of Sociology at the University of North Carolina at Chapel Hill, thank you. I am honored to be among such incredible scholars. And a sincere thank you to the UNC sociology graduate students I have had the pleasure of working with in my time at UNC as well—thank you not just for your help with the nuts and bolts of grading but for your collegiality and intellectual stimulation as well.

I would like to offer a final thank-you to my favorite sociologist, colleague, best friend, and partner, Tony Ladd. Your love and support sustain me. Your kind heart and keen intellect impress me daily. Your patience with my impatience is more than appreciated. Experiencing months of stay-at-home orders with you due to COVID-19 made me appreciate you even more—I love you!

Kathleen J. Fitzgerald
Department of Sociology
University of North Carolina at Chapel Hill
July 2020

SAGE wishes to thank the following reviewers for their valuable feedback during the development of this book:

Emile H. Hawkins Sr., Southeastern University

Alicia Smith Tran, Texas Christian University

Lori Waite, Tennessee Wesleyan University

Understanding Race, Racism, and the Racial Hierarchy

As I write this, in the midst of the COVID-19 pandemic, protesters fill the streets in all 50 states, in every major city and countless small towns, and in at least 18 countries across the globe, in reaction to the killing of a man racialized as Black, George Floyd, by a Minneapolis police officer, Derek Chauvin, a man racialized as White. Floyd was lying facedown on the concrete, handcuffed, as Chauvin knelt on his neck for 8 minutes and 46 seconds, and two fellow officers held his legs and lower back while a third kept the crowd at bay. Cell phone video clearly shows that for nearly the first 8 minutes, Floyd begged for his life, exclaiming, "I can't breathe, please," "you're going to kill me," and finally, pleading for his mother. During the last minute, he was motionless and unconscious. Police had originally been called to the scene because Floyd was suspected of passing a forged $20 bill. This was not the first killing of an unarmed person of color by a police officer, nor was it the first to be captured on cell phone video and shared with the world. But it is the first to inspire global rage against one of the primary forms of racial discrimination—police brutality—and particularly its manifestation in the United States (see Chapter 4).

We are bombarded with race stories daily, often in the media—from police killings of unarmed People of Color, like the story of George Floyd's murder, to photos of elected officials wearing blackface at college parties decades ago, to statistics showing the racial discrepancies in U.S. maternal mortality rates. Race informs all our lives, whether we are cognizant of it or not. For some people, that means being on the undesirable receiving end of racial discrimination. For others, it might mean not having to think much about race. It is hard to deny the ongoing significance of race in our society. And yet, in the post–civil rights era, a narrative emerged that proclaimed race no longer mattered—that race was merely a historical legacy in this country, carrying no significance today. When President Obama was elected in 2008, political media pundits immediately declared the U.S. a postracial society. Yet, eight years later, President Trump campaigned on an explicitly racist platform and won. How is it that two seemingly contradictory messages permeate our culture?

While some people try to convince us that race no longer matters, sociologists are under no such illusion. Sociologist Howard Winant (2015:313) goes so far as to argue that race and racism are the dark matter of the modern era, invisible yet possessing "mass and gravitational attraction." In the post–civil rights movement era, the dominant racial ideology, created and embraced primarily by people racialized as White, has been that of **colorblindness**, the idea that one does not see color and that race is no longer a significant influence in society or on one's life. Former Starbucks CEO Howard Schultz announced in a CNN town hall appearance, "I honestly don't see color." Such statements, which are most common among people racialized as White, are patently absurd. We all see color. We know when we walk into a room if we are the only person racialized as Black, or Latinx, or White. We make note of race in all our interactions, whether consciously or subconsciously.

So why would someone make such an absurd claim? Because Americans—and particularly those racialized as White—have been well socialized into the ideology of colorblindness, where we have been taught that seeing and acknowledging race is equivalent to racism. You see this when a person racialized as White describes a person racialized as Black and whispers their race, while speaking in a normal voice when listing other descriptors. ("He is the tall, *Black* guy on the stage.") You see it when a child racialized as White comments on the race of another person in a public space and the parent quickly shushes the child, sending a message of shame to the child for noticing differences in skin color. Sociologists Michael Omi and Howard Winant (1994:57) explain that according to the colorblind ideology, race "is not a morally valid basis upon which to treat people . . . We may notice someone's race, but we cannot act upon that awareness. We must act in a 'color-blind' fashion." For people racialized as non-White, the problem is not difference or the acknowledgment of difference; it is inequality—the fact that some people face discrimination and oppression based upon their race. There is a certain appeal to the colorblind ideology, as Omi and Winant (1994) note. The idea that no special rights, privileges, or disadvantages are attached to race aligns neatly with the American ideology of meritocracy. Unfortunately, it is not true. The United States has historically been and remains an extremely color-conscious society and inequality along racial lines remains prominent and is the focus of this book (Omi and Winant 1994).

Scholars argue that colorblindness manifests as **colorblind racism**, which explains contemporary racial inequality as an outcome of nonracial dynamics, for instance, as a result of market forces, naturally occurring phenomena, or Black cultural inferiority (Bonilla-Silva 2010). Compared to the Jim Crow era, which preceded the colorblind era, colorblind racism is often described as "racism lite," where "instead of proclaiming God placed minorities in the world in a servile position, it suggests they are behind because they do not work hard enough; instead of viewing interracial marriage as wrong on a straight racial basis, it regards it as 'problematic' because of concerns over the children" (Bonilla-Silva 2010:3). Colorblind racism reinforces the racial hierarchy and

White privilege, two concepts we introduce later in this chapter, by denying the ongoing significance of race in the post–civil rights era. People racialized as White are free to express their resentment of minorities by instead criticizing their morality or work ethic, ultimately employing a strategy Bonilla-Silva (2010) refers to as "racism without racists." The embrace of a colorblind society means that we pretend that "racial considerations . . . [are] never entertained in the selection of leaders, in hiring decisions, and the distribution of goods and services in general" (Omi and Winant 1994:117). In the end, embracing colorblindness reinforces the racial hierarchy and White supremacy.

Race and COVID-19

However, certain circumstances or events can shine a bright light on U.S. racism and make racial disparities glaringly visible, at least temporarily dismantling the power of the colorblind ideology. Police killings of unarmed People of Color fall under this category. How the COVID-19 pandemic has played out in the U.S. is also a good example of this. From the racial/ethnic disparities in health, to the racialized nature of the economic fallout from the social-distancing measures initially implemented to curb transmission of the virus, to the dramatic increase in anti-Asian prejudice and discrimination, to demands to reopen the economy, race is a defining feature of the pandemic.

In terms of racial/ethnic health disparities, people racialized as African American, Native American, and Latinx face disproportionate rates of infection, hospitalization, and mortality (Hummer 2020). COVID-19 hotspots, locations of the highest rates of infection, are predominantly low-income, African American neighborhoods (Godoy and Wood 2020). According to the Centers for Disease Control and Prevention, as of June 25, 2020, the COVID-19 hospitalization rate for people racialized as American Indian and Alaska Native was 5 times that of people racialized as non-Hispanic White; for people racialized as non-Hispanic Black, hospitalization rates were 5 times those racialized as non-Hispanic White; and people racialized as Hispanic or Latinx had 4 times the hospitalization rates of those racialized as non-Hispanic White ("COVID-19 in Racial Ethnic…" 2020) (see Figure 1.1).

Death rates for people racialized as Black are 2 times greater than expected based upon their population size. In some states, their death rates are 3 times greater. In California, people racialized as Latinx compose 53 percent of the COVID-19 cases, yet they make up just under 40 percent of the state's population (Branson-Potts, Reyes-Velarde, Stiles, and

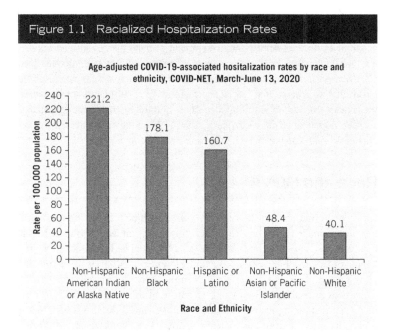

Figure 1.1   Racialized Hospitalization Rates

Age-adjusted COVID-19-associated hositalization rates by race and ethnicity, COVID-NET, March-June 13, 2020

Source: "COVID-19 in Racial and Ethnic Minority Groups." Centers for Disease Control and Prevention (CDC), June 25, 2020. https://www.cdc.gov/coronavirus/2019-ncov/need-extra-precautions/racial-ethnic-minorities.html

Campa 2020). As of May 18, 2020, the Navajo Nation surpassed the state of New York for highest COVID-19 infection rate in the U.S. (Silverman, Toropin, and Sidner 2020). There is also growing evidence that in North Carolina, people racialized as Latinx, particularly those who are non–English speakers, are being denied necessary hospitalization, a pattern likely found elsewhere (Bonner 2020).

There are a couple of inaccurate ways one could interpret the racial health discrepancies associated with COVID-19. One is to view race as biological and to assume there is something about racial minorities that makes them biologically more susceptible to COVID-19. Later in this chapter, we provide evidence that race is not biological, so this kind of an explanation does not withstand scrutiny. Unlike human beings, viruses actually are colorblind. A second misinterpretation, one that has gotten more traction in the media, is to argue that racial minorities put themselves at greater risk of infection and death from COVID-19 due to their behaviors—a blame-the-victim approach. For instance, the presence of certain comorbidities, such as diabetes and hypertension, increase one's risk of death from COVID-19, and people racialized as African American, Native American, and Latinx have disproportionately high rates of both.

Decades of sociological research instead places racism as the cause of racial health disparities, up to and including COVID-19 (Hummer 2020). Structural explanations for these racial health disparities include poverty, which increases the likelihood one lives in densely populated housing, making social distancing more difficult; being forced to continue working, thus increasing one's risk for contracting the virus and also increasing the risk of spreading it to a family member, since poor people are more likely to live in multigenerational households; having to rely on public transportation to get to one's job; and not having health insurance, which inhibits one's ability to get tested and treated. In addition, access to COVID-19 testing has been extremely limited in the U.S., with testing sites "disproportionately located in whiter communities" (Godoy and Wood 2020). Finally, people racialized as minorities are overrepresented in jails, prisons, and detention facilities, many of which have become COVID-19 hotspots.

Racial inequalities connected with COVID-19 extend beyond disparate health outcomes. Since COVID-19 is so contagious and there is no vaccine, the public health approach to controlling the epidemic has been to enforce social distancing—world leaders, mayors, and governors began enforcing stay-at-home orders during the early stages of the pandemic. This meant that thousands of businesses closed and furloughed or fired their employees, resulting in millions of people facing unemployment. In the United States, the unemployment rate hit nearly 14.7 percent in April, the highest since the Great Depression (Jan 2020). People racialized as Black and Hispanic were much more likely to face unemployment than those racialized as White and Asian American. In April of 2020, the unemployment rate for people racialized as Hispanic was 18.9 percent; for those racialized as African American, it was 16.7 percent; for people racialized as Asian American, it was 14.5 percent; and for those racialized as White, it was 14.2 percent. This was a dramatic increase in unemployment rates for all races, as prior to the shutdown, the rates were 4.4 percent for people racialized as Hispanic, 5.8 percent for people racialized as African American, 2.5 percent for people racialized as Asian American, and 3.1 percent for people racialized as White (Jan 2020; see Figure 1.2).

Unemployment rates for people racialized as Black have historically been double the unemployment rates for those racialized as White, and

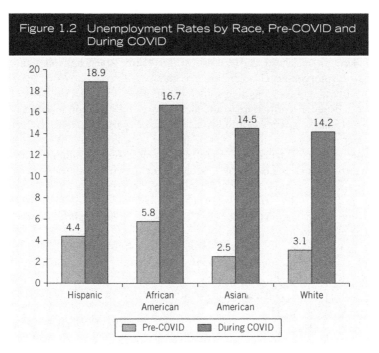

Figure 1.2 Unemployment Rates by Race, Pre-COVID and During COVID

Source: Jan, Tracy. 2020. "This Is How Economic Pain Is Distributed in America." The Washington Post May 9. Retrieved June 1, 2020. (https://www.washingtonpost.com/business/2020/05/09/jobs-report-demographics/).

economic recovery is generally slower for those racialized as Black (Jan 2020). Some data finds that adults racialized as Hispanic/Latinx were the hardest hit by wage and job losses. Specifically, in April of 2020, 62 percent of people racialized as Latinx and 44 percent of people racialized as Black said that either they or someone in their household had experienced job or wage loss due to the coronavirus, compared to 38 percent of adults racialized as White (Lopez, Rainie, and Budiman 2020). Part of the reason people racialized as White and Asian American have lower unemployment rates than those racialized as Black and Hispanic during the pandemic is because they are more likely to be in professions where they can work from home; thus, when stay-at-home orders were implemented throughout most of the country, more of them were able to continue working.

The situation for undocumented immigrants was particularly bleak because they slip through the federal safety net and do not qualify for food stamps, Medicaid, or subsidized housing, and they were not eligible to receive the $1,200.00 stimulus check the federal government provided for relief. Heidi Shierholz of the Economic Policy Institute explains that for undocumented immigrants, the human suffering is "much more dramatic" than unemployment statistics reveal (Jan 2020). The economic plight of people racialized as Native American during the pandemic was also dire. Approximately 40 percent of federally recognized tribes operate casinos, which were all closed due to the coronavirus (Mineo 2020).

While many businesses were forced to close, those deemed essential were required to remain open, and thus, those employees faced greater risk of infection. People racialized as non-White and immigrants are concentrated in many of the low-wage, low-status jobs that were deemed essential, such as grocery clerks, nursing home aides, janitors, truck drivers, and food processing plant employees (Branson-Potts et al. 2020; Kallberg 2020). In many of these jobs, maintaining social distancing was impossible, and personal protective equipment had been in short supply. Workers at a McDonald's in Monterey Park, California, walked off the job to protest their lack of "safety supplies, including masks, gloves, soap, and hand sanitizer" after a coworker was hospitalized with COVID-19 (Branson-Potts et al. 2020).

COVID-19 outbreaks in meatpacking plants, an industry that disproportionately relies on workers racialized as Latinx or Hispanic, throughout the U.S. have led to many small towns becoming hotspots; "at least 12 of the 25 hotspots in the US . . . originated in meat factories" (Lakhani 2020). As of May 15, 2020, 30 meatpacking plant workers have died from complications of COVID-19, and more than 10,000 workers have been infected or exposed to the coronavirus. Due to the outbreaks, dozens of plants suspended or reduced their operations, fueling threats of a meat shortage, until President Trump pressured them to reopen, declaring meat processing to be critical infrastructure (Lakhani 2020).

In addition to the pandemic's effect on human health and the economy, it has also resulted in increased anti-Asian prejudice and discrimination across the globe as people have blamed China for the origins of the epidemic. Some of this has been fueled by government leaders, including President Trump, who have referred to COVID-19 as "Kung flu" and the "Chinese virus," referencing its origins in the Wuhan Province of China. There are thousands of reported cases of people racialized as Asian American being harassed in public, both verbally and physically, and being denied services ("COVID-19 Fueling . . ." 2020). This has resulted in many people racialized as Asian in America wondering, many for the first time, whether they would ever truly belong in America (Cheung, Feng, and Deng 2020). We explore this in greater detail in Chapter 3 in our discussion of prejudice and stereotyping.

Finally, in the face of the economic crisis caused by the stay-at-home orders implemented throughout the country, in late April and early May, there was a push to reopen states, a movement composed almost exclusively of people racialized as White (Bouie 2020; Charles 2020). People racialized as White stormed state capitals, many of them armed with semi-automatic rifles and waved Confederate flags, refused to wear masks or practice social distancing, and demanded the freedom to get their haircuts. People racialized as White demanding that the economy reopen were operating on the assumption that they or people they love were unlikely to suffer the consequences, as COVID-19 had a disproportionate impact on People of Color (Reeves 2020). Some have argued that the goals of this movement are "rooted in a desire to return to their white dominance and white comfort" and a sense of White entitlement (Mallett 2020).

Confronting Racism

It is possible that the preceding discussion "raced" the pandemic in ways you had never thought about. If that is the case, it is likely due to the dominance of the colorblind ideology that pervades our society. While most Americans have been well socialized into colorblindness and the idea that we should not notice race, people racialized as White have been particularly susceptible to this narrative.

Due to this, many Americans—but especially those racialized as White—find talking about race and racism difficult. Have you ever found yourself in a situation where someone makes a comment that seems clearly racist, and you want to challenge it but do not quite know how? Or maybe the comment made you feel uncomfortable, but you felt it was not your responsibility to challenge it because it was not directed at you or your racial group. Many people do not have the tools to speak about race eloquently and, thus, avoid challenging racism. Or maybe you have called out perpetrators of racist comments in the past, only to find their anger and hostility at being called on their racism scared you; so you sit in silence in the face of the current comment. That anger and hostility at being called out on one's racism is a phenomenon that Robin DiAngelo (2018) identifies as **White fragility**, overreacting emotionally by getting angry and upset, claiming to feel overwhelming guilt, and overreacting behaviorally by arguing, retreating in silence, or walking away from the situation whenever one is faced with racial stressors.

This book is designed to provide you with a foundation for understanding race and communicating these ideas by introducing you to the basic terms, concepts, debates, and theories social scientists use to understand our racialized world. This knowledge will allow you to identify White fragility and racism when you see them and have the tools to address them. Moving forward, this chapter explores the racial status hierarchy, an understanding of race privilege, racial inequality, and intersectionality. Our analysis then shifts to understanding the social construction of race, ethnicity, and racism.

Racial Status Hierarchy

All societies have developed **status hierarchies**, where one group is dominant and therefore receives benefits and privileges related to power and resources that the other group or groups are either denied or have limited access to. Groups exist on a hierarchy—some at the top, some in the middle, while others are at the bottom. Sociologists use the terms **dominant** or **majority group** to describe those groups at the top of the hierarchy—those that have more than their proportionate share of society's goods or resources. The terms **subordinate** or **minority group** refer to disadvantaged groups—those at the bottom of the racial hierarchy who have less than their proportionate share of society's goods and resources. The sociological use of *majority* and *minority* differs from the mathematical understanding of those terms. We are not referring to group size; instead, we are referring to the groups' differing access to power and resources. There are many situations where the statistical majority (the larger group) is a sociological minority (the disadvantaged group). For instance, in the United States, women make up 51 percent of the population yet are a minority group because women earn less than men, are underrepresented politically, and are disproportionately targeted for sexual harassment and violence, among other things. South Africa under apartheid is another example of a society where the statistical minority group was the dominant group. Apartheid, which means "separate," was the legal system of segregation in South Africa between 1948 and 1994 (see Chapter 6). Under this racial hierarchy, the statistical minority, people racialized as White, held disproportionate power and access to resources, while people racialized as Black and/or "Coloured" were discriminated against and disadvantaged economically, politically, and socially. Extreme racial inequality remains as a legacy of apartheid; in 2011, people racialized as White composed only 8 percent of the population, those racialized as Black Africans composed 80 percent, 9 percent were people racialized as "Coloured," 2 percent were people racialized as Indian or Asian, and 1 percent were classified as "other" (Knaus and Brown 2016:11).

Every society has multiple status hierarchies, including a gender hierarchy, where men or people perceived to be men are the dominant group and women or those perceived to be women are disadvantaged. In addition to gender, there are status hierarchies linked to social class, sexuality, ability, age, and nationality, among others. This book is going to focus on the **racial hierarchy**, where people racialized as White people are the dominant group, the group that benefits from the racial status hierarchy, and those racialized as People of Color are disadvantaged by that same status hierarchy; people racialized as Black are on the bottom rung of the racial hierarchy, with other racial minority groups existing between Whites and Blacks. There are two important things to remember about status hierarchies: First, it is equally important to understand what groups *benefit* from these hierarchies and what that looks like as it is to investigate and expose how groups are *disadvantaged* by the hierarchy and how that disadvantage manifests. Second, status hierarchies intersect with one another, creating new and different forms of disadvantage, a phenomenon referred to as intersectionality (discussed later).

White Privilege

Social scientists use the term **White privilege** to capture the myriad ways people perceived as White are advantaged by the racial status hierarchy—the unearned benefits and advantages one accrues simply by being perceived as White. The concept of White privilege shifts our attention away from those who are disadvantaged by societal status hierarchies, from those who experience the brunt of racism, and toward those who are advantaged by the system. It means that there is no neutrality in a racialized social system—it means either you are disadvantaged by it or you are advantaged, but no one exists outside the system.

White privilege manifests in concrete, tangible ways. One way is economically in the form of a **racial wage gap**, where Americans racialized as White earn more than those racialized as Black, Native American, and Latinx, even with the same education, skills, and experience (see Chapter 4). Our previous discussion of the pandemic shows that social distancing can also be understood as a privilege, one that falls along race and class lines. The most concrete manifestation of White privilege, however, is life expectancy. In the United States, life expectancy for Black men is 72 years, which is four years less than White men, seven years less than Black women, and an astonishing nine years less than White women (Kendi 2019). Historian Ibram X. Kendi poignantly asserts, "There may be no more consequential privilege than life itself. The privilege of being on the living end of racism" (Kendi 2019).

iStockphoto.com/SolStock

The most significant manifestation of White privilege may be life itself; people racialized as White have longer life expectancies than those racialized as People of Color.

White privilege is evident in any one of the numerous recent stories of people racialized as White calling the police on people racialized as Black who are just going about their daily routines and is evidence of the "pervasive phenomenon of Black bodies being policed for being 'out of place'" (Howell, Skoczylas, and DeVaughn 2019). This happens so much that terms and memes capturing it have emerged; women racialized as White who have an exaggerated sense of entitlement are referred to as "BBQ Beckys" or "Karens." A female African American student at Yale, Lolade Siyonbola, fell asleep in her dorm lounge after working late on papers. The next morning, a student racialized as White found her there and proceeded to call campus police, while telling Siyonbola she was not allowed to sleep there. The numerous examples of people racialized as White calling the police on people racialized as Black who are simply going about their daily lives are certainly examples of racial discrimination against minorities, but they are also examples of White privilege. In these examples, people racialized as White feel a sense of entitlement to a space and, simultaneously, assume anyone racialized as non-White does not belong and must be an intruder. It is also an exercise of White privilege in that people racialized as White calling the police on people racialized as Black they encounter in their daily life never assume there will be any backlash for calling the police on an innocent person. Not only do they not assume that they will be charged with filing a false police report, they are also comfortable enough not to imagine the entire scene turning sour, where they will be the target of violent actions by the police officer. This is something less imaginable for people racialized as Black or Brown.

Another way privilege manifests is in the freedom to travel. Part of the American lore includes a romanticized version of freedom and the "open road." As a college student, you may experience this in the form of spontaneous road trips with friends or have experienced it in the form of family vacations when you were a child. The freedom of the open road is so engrained in our cultural imagination that it might be hard for you to see this as an example of White privilege. Yet people racialized as African American have not always had the same freedom to enjoy the open road. During slavery, the mobility of people racialized as Black was constrained by laws. But even after emancipation, Black mobility was limited for generations. In many parts of the Jim Crow south, laws that prohibited people racialized as Black from traveling existed. But even outside the South, opportunities for people racialized as Black to travel were restricted by the limited number of hotels, restaurants, and gas stations that would cater to clientele racialized as Black, as well as by the threat of violence on the road (Taylor 2020).

In reaction to this, a New York City mail carrier, Victor Hugo Green, published a travelers' guide for Americans racialized as Black in 1936 titled *The Negro Motorist Green Book*, which was changed to *Negro Travelers' Green Book* in 1959, to help people racialized as Black navigate Jim Crow and discrimination in America. In the 1949 edition of the book, the author optimistically stated, "There will be a day sometime in the future when this guide will not have to be published. That is when we as a race will have equal opportunities and privileges in the United States" (Green 1949). The significance of this publication cannot be overstated. Author Candacy Taylor (2020:11, 13) explains, "The *Green Book* was published during a time when car travel symbolized freedom in America, but since racial segregation was in full force throughout the country, the open road was not open to all . . . [The *Green Book*] was an ingenious solution to a horrific problem."

While there is no longer a need for a *Green Book*, people racialized as African American still do not share the freedom to travel equally with Whites. A recent report from Missouri's attorney general finds that drivers racialized as Black are 91 percent more likely to be pulled over by police than drivers racialized as White in Missouri. This is true even in communities where they live (Ballantine 2019). Due to this, in 2017, the NAACP issued a travel advisory warning people racialized as Black to be

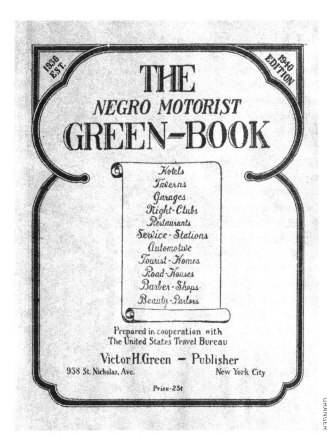

GRANGER

The *Green Book* was published from 1936–1966 to help African Americans navigate travel as safely as possible during the Jim Crow era, where it was legal for businesses to refuse to serve African Americans.

extra careful when traveling in Missouri (Ballantine 2019). In Ferguson, Missouri, a small suburb in St. Louis's North County where uprisings against the police killing of an unarmed teen racialized as Black, Michael Brown, in August 2014 generated national attention, drivers racialized as Black that same year were 265 percent more likely to be pulled over than motorists racialized as White (Ballantine 2019).

Intersectionality

While this text will primarily focus on the racial hierarchy, status hierarchies do not operate in isolation. Instead, they intersect, interact, and influence one another, at times compounding experiences of inequality and at other times creating entirely distinct forms of inequality, something social scientists refer to as **intersectionality** (Crenshaw 1989; Grzanka 2014). As Kimberlé Crenshaw (1989) articulates, women racialized as Black sometimes experience discrimination as *Black* people (similar to what men racialized as Black face), sometimes as *women* (similar to what women racialized as White face), while other times they face discrimination as *Black women* (cumulative or unique types of discrimination associated with being gendered as a woman *and* being racialized as Black). The idea of intersectionality recognizes that as status hierarchies intersect with one another, individuals can experience unique forms of discrimination that are a result of their multiple statuses, for instance, being Black and a woman.

A good example of the intersection of race and class is offered by Kendi (2019b) in his concept of **race-classes** which are racial groups that exist at the intersection of the race and class status hierarchies. This idea is quite familiar, even if one had not thought to refer to it in this way. For instance, the idea of "White trash," a derogatory term for poor people racialized as White, captures this idea of race-classes quite well. Similarly, "ghetto Blacks" is a negative reference to poor people racialized as Black.

Another example of intersectionality can be found in the disturbing epidemic of lethal violence against transgender women of color (Fitzgerald 2017). Record numbers of transgender women racialized as Black or Latinx

iStockphoto.com/FatCamera

Intersectionality encourages us to recognize how intersecting systems of oppression lead to new and different forms of discrimination; this woman has likely experienced discrimination as a woman, as a Black person, as an elderly person, and as various intersections of those identities.

have been violently murdered since 2012. At first glance, this might appear to be a result of **transphobia**, the fear and hatred of transgender individuals based upon their gender expression and nonconformity. Or maybe these actions appear to qualify as examples of **misogyny**, the fear, hatred, and denigration of women, girls, and all things feminine (Kacere 2014). However, the fact that the violence is overwhelmingly directed at transwomen racialized as Black or Brown implores us to recognize these crimes as something else; they should be understood as **racialized transmisogyny**, the negative attitudes toward and discrimination against transwomen and gender nonconforming people racialized as Black or Brown. It is not just that they are transgender or that they are female or that they are racialized as non-White but the intersection of these oppressions that creates racialized transmisogyny and is resulting in their disproportionate rates of lethal violent victimization.

The Origins of Race

Now that we have established that race is one of multiple, intersecting status hierarchies, we shift our discussion to understanding race and how it became such a significant social category. This requires an understanding of the term *race*, the origins of the concept of race, and what is meant by the claim that race is a social construction. **Race** is a socially constructed category that refers to people grouped together based on physical appearance (skin color, facial features, and hair texture) and is treated as if it has biological validity. It is a concept that "signifies and symbolizes social conflicts and interests by referring to different types of human bodies" (Omi and Winant 1994:55). The concept of race differs from that of **ethnicity** or **ethnic group**, which refers to a group of people who share certain cultural characteristics, such as language, ancestry, and religion (see Chapter 2).

Everyone has a race and an ethnicity, yet we tend to overlook the ethnicity of people racialized as minorities, such as the fact that a person racialized as Black can be a descendent of people enslaved in the United States generations ago, or be of Jamaican descent, or a Nigerian immigrant to the United States. All of those people are perceived as Black in the United States and presumed to share experiences based upon their Blackness, yet they have very different ethnicities, which also significantly inform their life experiences. In the U.S., we downplay the ethnicity of people racialized as racial minorities and overemphasize their race. The opposite is true for people racialized as White. In this case, there is more often an emphasis on their ethnicity and a downplaying of their race. People racialized as

White with Irish ancestry, for instance, generally refer to themselves by their ethnicity (Irish American) yet fail to mention their race (White). This is an example of White privilege; the fact that Whiteness is the norm, the assumed race unless otherwise mentioned.

The use of the language "racialized as Black" and "racialized as White" in this book is intentional. It is meant to make us think more deeply about racial categories and identities and to recognize them as social constructions (a concept explored in more detail later in this chapter). Racial categorization is a result of a **racialization process**, a process whereby a group is assigned a place in the racial hierarchy (Omi and Winant 1994). Keeping this front and center during our discussion of race, racism, and privilege is essential.

The ultimate racialization process was the creation of race itself. The world has not always been raced; dividing people up along the lines of physical appearance is a product of the intersection of colonialism and capitalism. As Europeans traveled the globe and encountered indigenous peoples of various continents that were new to them, their desire to exploit these new lands, people, and resources resulted in their defining them as uncivilized, inferior heathens. The emergence of the global slave trade created the previously unheard-of racial categories of "White" and "Black." Importantly, ideologies of the inferiority of people racialized as Black emerged to justify slavery; people racialized as Black were not enslaved because they were perceived to be inferior.

The Social Construction of Race

While we live in a culture that has treated race as biologically real for several centuries, race is instead a **social construction**. To say something is socially constructed is to emphasize that there is no biological basis to this categorization system; instead, society assigns meaning to certain physical characteristics. The idea of race was socially created for the benefit of some groups and at the expense of others, beginning in the colonial era and continuing through the current era. The claim that race is a social construction probably challenges what you think you see every day and what you have learned your entire life. After all, for most of us, we have internalized the idea that race is "real" and that it is something we can see with our own eyes.

Social scientists encourage you to put aside this commonsense understanding of race and look at the evidence that it is a social construction. The first piece of evidence that race is a social construction comes from what we know about the human genome itself. Scientists announced the results of the Human Genome Project in 2000, finding that human beings are 99.9 percent genetically similar; thus, there is no empirical, biological basis to the racial categories humans have created. To put it another way, there is no genetic marker that is found in all people of a so-called race and not found in anyone from another so-called racial group.

The fact that the idea of race originated in a specific time period, discussed previously, and thus that there was a time when the idea of breaking human beings up into hierarchical groups based upon physical appearance did not exist is also evidence that race is a social construction. If race were biologically real, we would not be able to establish its origins in time. Race would be a concept as old as humanity itself, yet this is not the case.

Another piece of evidence that shows us that racial categories are social constructions has to do with the fact that racial categories change over time and place. If you look at the U.S. census, for instance, you will see that racial categories have always been in flux. The Census Bureau debated whether to add "Hispanic" and "MENA," a category that refers to Middle Eastern and North African, as racial categories on the 2020 census, but it ultimately declined. In the past, racial categories included "mulatto," "octoroon," "quadroon," "Negro," "Oriental," and "non-White," none of which are part of our census racial category options today. Certain groups, such as Irish, Jewish, Greeks, Armenians, and Italians, who are now viewed as unquestionably White were once understood as non-White. Keep in mind that nothing about the appearance of these people changed, yet at some point in time, their group's racial categorization did change. Racialization is an ongoing negotiation, which means that the place a group is assigned in the racial hierarchy may change, as the prior examples of groups formerly understood as non-White and who are now viewed as White exemplify.

Racial categories not only change across time but also across place. If you study race across cultures, you will find that someone defined as "White" in Brazil can move to the United States, where they might not be defined as "White" (see Chapter 6). Again, keep in mind that nothing about these people's physical appearance has changed—they simply moved from one culture to another and, in that process, encountered a different racial context. Racial categorization systems vary across cultures because they are politically contested and historically contingent.

Racial categories can also vary within cultures. For instance, in the early 1900s, in California, Mexican Americans were referred to as Mexican-Indian to distinguish them from Mexicans of European, specifically Spanish, descent. This occurred even though, at the same time, the federal government referred to Mexicans as White (Clark 1918; Digernes 2020). Sociologists speak of the sociohistorical process where racial categories are created, inhabited, transformed, and destroyed as **racial formations** (Omi and Winant 1994).

Another piece of evidence that shows race is a social construction rather than a biological reality is that there is more physical and genetic variation within a so-called racial group than between two so-called racial groups. If you line up 100 randomly selected people (or just the students in your sociology lecture hall) by skin color, from lightest to darkest, you will likely discover that there are people racialized as White who have darker skin than some who are racialized as Black. The reverse is true as well; some people racialized as Black can be lighter-skinned than people who are racialized as White. How does this make sense if racial categorization is based upon phenotype, principally skin color? It shows us that the racial categorization system is a socially created—and flawed—concept.

Finally, the presence of biracial and multiracial people is also evidence of the arbitrary nature of our racial categorization system. Until the 2000 census, for instance, biracial and multiracial people in the United States had to identify as one race on official documents like the census (see Chapter 5). For many people, if not most, checking the race box on a census or on standardized test forms or any other official document is unproblematic. For many others, however, this situation was fraught with tension. The racial categories biracial and multiracial people have had to choose from have not accurately represented who they are. Additionally, it was not like they had complete freedom to just choose whatever race they wanted. While people with multiracial ancestry have long existed, due to centuries of miscegenation (racial mixing, voluntary or forced), their White ancestry has generally been ignored, denied, or overlooked. This norm used to be ensconced in law, something known as the **one-drop rule**, which required that a person with any amount of Black ancestry, no matter how minimal, was racialized as Black. This was more broadly applied as the **hypodescent rule**, in which a racially mixed person is assigned the race of the subordinate group member (Harris 1964; Davis 1991). The one-drop rule was codified as law during slavery as a way to make sure children born to a slave woman and fathered by the White master would count as slaves, as property, and not attempt to claim their White heritage and the privilege of freedom associated with that.

Arguing that race is a social construction should not be interpreted to mean that race is insignificant; race matters considerably in our world today. Race is a significant determinant of your life expectancy, whether you feel comfortable enough to take a road trip, the neighborhood you live in, your educational opportunities, and your income, among other things. Race is highly significant. But it is not biological.

Racism

We end this chapter with an introduction to racism, which is explored in detail throughout the book. **Racism** can be defined as both the

> explicit and implicit beliefs and acts that justify the assertion of power—individually, collectively, or systemically—against racially maligned people and their white allies, so as to minimize their freedom, access to resources, and sense of value in the world . . . deep and pervasive cultural conditioning for grouping others into categories and placing them at enough distance to render their suffering less visible, for obscuring our intertwined destinies, and for turning us *against* one another rather than *toward* one another (Magee 2019:14, 16).

This lengthy definition best captures the complexity of racism; it encompasses both beliefs and actions; it can be enacted by individuals, groups, or systemically; it is designed to limit minority groups' access to resources and their overall freedom; it is deeply engrained in us through ongoing cultural conditioning and socialization; and it succeeds in rendering the pain of subordinate groups invisible to dominant-group members. The function of racism is to justify and maintain the racial hierarchy and White supremacy.

We most often think of the malignant forms of racism, when we think about it at all. An example of this would be explicit violence and oppression, such as the brutal murder of James Byrd, who was chained to a vehicle and dragged to his death by White supremacists in 1998 in Jasper, Texas. Racism can also take more benign forms. Cultural racism, paternalism, and microaggressions fall into this category and constitute what some call the *new racism* (see Chapter 3). **Microaggressions**, a term that refers to commonplace, even daily, indirect, subtle, often unintentional instances of verbal discrimination or environmental indignities that communicate hostility to people racialized as racial/ethnic minorities, are also examples of individual discrimination. An example of a common microaggression is mispronouncing an international student's name and making no effort to learn the correct pronunciation. **Cultural racism** is the foundational idea behind colorblind racism, explaining racial disparities as a result of cultural deficiencies rather than as a result of racism. Racism changes in response to cultural changes; just because racism today is less likely to resemble racism of the Jim Crow era does not mean racism has disappeared.

In a culture that denigrates Blackness and venerates Whiteness, it is perhaps unsurprising to see that racism can also manifest within racial minority groups, as well as between them. This type of racism is referred to as **colorism**, the privileging of light skin over dark skin (Hunter 2005; Khanna 2020; Walker 1983). Colorism has long been practiced within the African American community, where lighter-skinned people racialized as Black are privileged. During the Jim Crow era, many clubs and organizations, from Black sororities and fraternities to churches and social clubs, discriminated against darker-skinned people racialized as Black by declining membership or admittance to people whose skin was darker than a paper bag. People racialized as White also have a history of showing favoritism toward lighter-skinned people racialized as Black in many ways, including through employment opportunities and perceptions of trustworthiness (Herring, Keith, and Horton 2005; Khanna 2020). Colorism is found across the globe, within and between Asian countries, throughout Latin America, and in the U.S. Latinx community. As sociologist Nikki Khanna explains, "Preference for light skin is deeply rooted both in Asian ethnic cultures and in European colonization . . . throughout Asia, light skin typically functions as a marker for wealth and class, caste, and proximity to whiteness" (Khanna 2020:9). Skin-lightening products are a multibillion-dollar business globally because of colorism. Colorism is an extension of racism and can be understood as "cousins or as parent and child—distinctly different, not nonetheless related" (Khanna 2020:4).

Toward a More Racially Just Society

This book is written from the perspective that racial justice should be a societal goal. That goal pedagogically informs this section, found at the end of each chapter, on the path toward a more racially just society. This is an opportunity to talk about some existing racial justice work, as well as work that remains to be done. Racial justice work must occur on two levels: internally, where we work on ourselves, and systemically, where we work to make organizations, institutions, and societies more just.

The internal work begins with education, but it must go deeper than that. It involves looking deeply and honestly at ourselves to understand the role race, racism, and privilege play in our lives, which is not easy; "a big part of racial justice work is about becoming more comfortable with being uncomfortable" (Magee 2019:28). As you learn more, you sit with what you are learning, sit with the discomfort, and commit to change. It appears that in this moment, Americans are embracing the call to become more educated on these topics. As the uprisings against the murder of George Floyd by a Minneapolis police officer spread across the globe, by early June

2020, the *New York Times* list of best-selling nonfiction books contained all titles related to racism, racial violence, and White privilege for the first time ever (Ward 2020). The same was true for the bestsellers at Amazon and Barnes & Noble (Harris 2020). Scholar and author Ibram X. Kendi, who had two books on the top-10 list during early June, said he hopes this surge in interest is about more than shame and guilt; he hopes that people understand reading these books to be "the beginning of a journey of a lifetime" so that we can one day live in a world that is antiracist (Harris 2020).

A book like this plays a role in educating people about the extent of racism and White privilege and, thus, is a necessary starting point. However, Kendi (2019b) argues that education alone will never bring about racial justice. He argues that we must understand that racism is about self-interest; the dominant group has a long history of establishing racist policies, then providing racist ideologies to justify them. Thus, he argues, the solution to racial inequality is policymaking. In the spirit of his advice, the path to racial justice is more than learning about race and racism. It is about looking around your world, the organizations and institutions in which you are embedded, and working to make those spaces more racially just by forcing policy changes.

A Note on Language

I made some editorial decisions in terms of language use in this text that I want to address up front, since language not only describes but helps create reality. First, I chose to use the language "racialized as *x*" instead of just saying Black or White or whatever race. While this can admittedly be a bit clunky upon first encountering such language, I believe it is more accurate and helps keep the idea that race is socially constructed front and center in our minds. The standard convention of using the language Black, White, or Brown problematically reifies race, something that I hope to avoid by instead using the words "racialized as . . ."

Second, I chose to follow the increasingly common convention of capitalizing Black when referring to people and communities of African origin. The *New York Times* and the *Washington Post* each announced they were implementing such a policy in July of 2020, just as I was finishing up this manuscript. I break with the *Times* and follow the *Post* on whether to capitalize White when referring to White people and White communities. I have chosen to capitalize White. I do this because this helps us recognize that White is an identity, a race, and a culture. White privilege has made this, ironically, hard to see; the fact that we are literally immersed in

Whiteness too often remains unacknowledged. I have additionally chosen to capitalize Brown when referring to other communities of color, such as Latinx communities. This is a less standard practice, but I think it adds a consistency to the book and serves to recognize and humanize communities and people racialized as Brown. While often seen as Brown, Latinxs are a racially diverse group, with some identifying as White while others identify as Black or Afro-Latinx, thus complicating the picture. Additionally, many of my Native American and South Asian students over the years have referred to themselves as Brown. I hope using the term *Brown* captures how so many of them see themselves, despite the potential limitations of this terminology. The terms we use to describe racial/ethnic groups are social constructions and, as such, are often problematic. In that spirit, I assume my editorial choices will not please everyone.

A third editorial decision I made pertained to the use of the language Asian American. When U.S. racial data is collected and reported, Asians in America are referred to simply as Asian. I find this troubling and fear it risks perpetually Othering them, fueling the idea that they are forever foreigners, a long-standing anti–Asian American stereotype. The term *African American* clearly denotes the Americanness of the person, as does the term *Native American*; while both are still somewhat problematic in other ways, there is no question the terms are referring to people in the United States. The terms *Hispanic* and *Latinx* are used interchangeably to refer to Americans who come from or whose ancestors descend from Spain or Latin America; the terms do not distinguish between immigrants or natural-born citizens. Yet the term *Asian* does the opposite; it implies they are not Americans. I opt to use the phrase *Asian American*, which simply refers to people who come from or whose ancestors descend from Asian countries, whether they are immigrants or natural-born citizens and whether the original data collection referred to them only as Asian.

Conclusion

This chapter begins with evidence of the ongoing significance of race, racism, and privilege in our lives, despite the dominant cultural ideology of colorblindness, from police killings of unarmed People of Color to the COVID-19 pandemic. It then explores the idea of societal status hierarchies, with attention paid to the racial hierarchy, and emphasizes not just that some groups are discriminated against by such hierarchies but that others are privileged; they benefit from the inequality. We then introduce some of the foundational ideas associated with the sociology of race and ethnicity, from a short discussion of the origins of race, to definitions of key terms, evidence of the social construction of race, and an introduction to racism and colorism. We conclude the chapter with a discussion of the role of education and policy changes that can help us move toward a more racially just society.

KEY TERMS AND CONCEPTS

Colorblindness   2
Colorblind racism   2
Colorism   20
Cultural racism   19
Dominant/majority group   9
Ethnicity/ethnic group   15
Hypodescent rule   18
Intersectionality   14
Microaggressions   19
Misogyny   15
One-drop rule   18
Race   15
Race-classes   14

Racial formation   18
Racial hierarchy   10
Racialization process   16
Racialized transmisogyny   15
Racial wage gap   10
Racism   19
Status hierarchy   9
Social construction   16
Subordinate/minority group   9
Transphobia   15
White fragility   8
White privilege   10

CRITICAL THINKING QUESTIONS

1. Apply the definition of racism found on page 19 to the chapter coverage of race and COVID-19. How many ways can you see racism play out in the pandemic? Reflect on the definition of racism; in what ways does this definition challenge how you thought about racism?

2. Read over the five pieces of evidence that show race is a social construction. Make a similar argument, using similar explanations, for other socially constructed categorizations, such as gender or sexuality. What is powerful about understanding these ideas as socially constructed? What opportunities does the idea that these are social constructions offer?

3. Outline five key ingredients that are necessary for a racially just society, in your opinion. What is the best path forward to attain the goal of a racially just society?

RECOMMENDED READINGS ─────────

Bonilla-Silva, Eduardo. 2010. *Racism Without Racists: Color-Blind Racism and Racial Inequality in Contemporary America*, 3rd Edition. Boulder, CO: Rowman and Littlefield Publishers.

Kendi, Ibram X. 2019. *How to Be an Antiracist*. New York: One World.

Khanna, Nikki. 2020. *Whiter: Asian American Women on Skin Color and Colorism*. New York: New York University Press.

Magee, Rhonda V. 2019. *The Inner Work of Racial Justice: Healing Ourselves and Transforming Our Communities Through Mindfulness*. New York: A Tarcherperigee Book.

Omi, Michael and Howard Winant. 1994. *Racial Formation in the United States: From the 1960s to the 1990s*, 2nd Edition. New York: Routledge.

Rothenberg, Paula. 2015. *White Privilege: Essential Readings on the Other Side of Racism*, 5th Edition. New York: Worth Publishers.

Immigration, Assimilation, Ethnicity, and Race

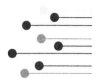

The U.S. national narrative that we learn in elementary school is that we are a nation of immigrants; people from across the globe come to the United States to embrace opportunities that simply do not exist elsewhere; they are welcomed, work hard, and become American. The term most often used to describe this process is that it is a "melting pot"—diverse people come here and melt into something new and unique, that of the American (McLemore and Romo 2005). There is some truth to this, obviously. For many people, this narrative captures their family history perfectly. But there are also limitations to this "melting pot" narrative. Is this idea applicable to people who are racialized as non-White, or does it only apply to those racialized as White, those with European ancestry? This chapter explores the melting pot narrative surrounding immigration, which is rooted in an assimilationist paradigm, as well as the critiques of it, the sociological literature on ethnicity, and we conclude with a discussion of the current and historic practice of racializing immigrants.

Early sociological research in the United States during the last decade of the nineteenth century and the first half of the twentieth overwhelmingly focused on ethnicity instead of race. This was partially due to different understandings of those terms during the first half of the nineteenth century—for instance, the idea that race was part of ethnicity, which we discuss in more detail later. As defined in Chapter 1, the term *ethnic group* refers to a group of people who share certain cultural characteristics, such as language, customs, and religion, among others. As scholar Werner Sollors (1996) explains, an ethnic group designates both a general peoplehood and an otherness; so ethnic minorities are both a part of and distinct from mainstream culture. Ethnicity is distinct from race, which refers to a group of people who share certain socially designated physical characteristics, such as skin color, hair texture, and facial features. And, of course, ethnicity and race are related and best expressed through the concept of racial/ethnic, the idea that everyone has a race and an ethnicity (see Chapter 1).

The term *ethnicity* is of much more recent origin than the term *race*. In the early twentieth century, social scientists speculated that the term ethnicity would replace the term *race*, which was perceived as compromised by racism (Sollors 1996). However, the term *ethnicity* has not come to replace *race*, either in the social sciences or in popular vernacular, perhaps because, as sociologists Omi and Winant (1994) point out, conflating race and ethnicity requires us to unacceptably overlook the unique historical oppression of racial minorities. Indeed, "the they-ness imputed to racial minorities by the dominant American

The United States's national narrative includes pride in its immigrant history, yet not all immigrant groups have been equally welcomed and xenophobic attitudes long existed.

society has been qualitatively different from the they-ness imputed to white ethnic minorities" (Ringer and Lawless 1989).

The overwhelming focus of sociological research on ethnicity at the exclusion of race is also because White sociologists of the era, led by Robert Ezra Park of the Chicago School of Sociology, promoted the **ethnicity paradigm**, the idea that race was simply part of ethnicity but that it was less important to people's lives than ethnicity. Such a claim seems more than a little tone-deaf considering this was the era of violent Jim Crow racism, including segregation, lynchings, and race riots. However, the Chicago School's understanding of race was progressive for the time in that they argued that race was socially constructed, rather than biological, which put them at odds with the dominant scientific thought of the era on the subject of race, which is captured by the science of eugenics. Despite these relatively progressive views, Park believed in Black cultural inferiority but resisted the dominant belief in Black biological inferiority.

It also must be acknowledged that institutional racism within academia and the discipline of sociology are also explanations for the dearth of research on race and racism and a narrow focus on ethnicity in the first half of the twentieth century. African American sociologist W. E. B. DuBois was a prolific scholar, researching and writing about race and racism during this era, yet he and his contributions were disregarded by mainstream members of the discipline (Morris 2015). The discipline of sociology was dominated by White men who did not perceive race and racism to be worthy topics of investigation. As sociologist Aldon D. Morris (2015:3) confirms, "white social scientists concurred with the general white consensus that blacks were created inferior and incapable of functioning as social equals of whites. For them, genetics and culture, rather than social conditions, produced racial inequality." Again, to describe the mainstream sociological attention to ethnicity and not race as more than a little tone-deaf during the Jim Crow era is an understatement.

The Assimilationist Paradigm

The dominant perspective pertaining to race/ethnicity in the field of sociology, as well as the United States at large, has been **assimilationism**, which literally translates to "to make more similar"; it refers to the process by which immigrants drop their ties to their culture of origin and adapt to the values, beliefs, and behaviors of their new culture. In theory, assimilation is a process that results in each subsequent generation experiencing upward social mobility through continued integration into the dominant society. The discipline of sociology has three primary theoretical perspectives, and assimilationism is an outgrowth of one of those perspectives: functionalism. Functionalists emphasize social order and harmony in society; thus, anything that can limit conflict is viewed as beneficial and desirable. When it comes to racial/ethnic diversity, functionalists push assimilation as beneficial because if groups become more similar, there will be less basis for conflict.

Beyond the discipline of sociology, it is easy to see the prominence of assimilationism in our culture as well. For instance, when Americans critique Muslim immigrant women for wearing a hijab, niqab, or burka, different types of coverings that many Muslim women wear, they are pressuring them to assimilate into the dominant culture, which is not only American but also White and Christian, emphasizing that such coverings are out of place within the mainstream culture. When Americans demand that immigrants "speak English!", they are showing the dominance of assimilationism in American society, as immigrants are expected to drop their ties to their culture of origin and become American. Immigrants do seek to assimilate. Some do so immediately through "Americanizing" their names, adapting their attire to match that of their new culture, and learning English. As sociologist Ronald Takaki (1993:298) explains, the "price of admission" into American society for immigrants is that they give up certain customs and traits that tie them to their ethnicity. Scholars who proposed the assimilationist paradigm, discussed later, understand assimilation is a process and does not happen overnight, whereas comments like the previous ones neglect to recognize assimilation as a process that takes time to complete.

Park's Race Relations Cycle

The origins of the discipline of sociology in the U.S. are deeply intertwined with the Chicago School of Sociology, particularly the years 1915 to 1935.[1] Research out of the Chicago School of Sociology focused on the experiences of European immigrants, who were racialized as White, using the city of Chicago as their lab. One of the most famous examples of the Chicago School's focus on White ethnics was W. I. Thomas and Florian Znaniecki's (1918–1920) *The Polish Peasant in Europe and America*.

This work and others influenced Chicago sociologist Robert Ezra Park (1950) to introduce his **race relations cycle**, which became the most influential assimilationist perspective in sociology. The race relations cycle explains four stages of contact between groups that encounter each other through migration: contact, competition, accommodation, and assimilation. The arrival of a new group of immigrants to an area is, obviously, going to create some competition—for jobs, housing, and schools, to name a few. This competition will result in conflict between the groups. Since conflict is undesirable for a society, the conflict will require accommodation, which refers to making the relationship between the groups stable through their institutionalization. Once social relations are institutionalized, attitudes develop that support the institutionalized relationship between the groups. Accommodation can and often does mean that the relationship between the groups is one of institutionalized inequality. While the accommodation stage can last for a long time, it eventually leads to assimilation, according to Park. Assimilation is the desired goal because Park saw that as "leading ultimately to universal participation in a common life and culture" (Cornell and Hartmann 1998:6).

The critiques of Park's race relations cycle are numerous. First, the use of the word *race* rather than *ethnicity* in the title is problematic, since it was never applied to the experiences of racial minorities, only to White ethnic immigrants. In his defense, Park "wrote at a time when *race* had a broader meaning than it does now. Park's conception of 'races' treated separately, for example, the Slavic peoples, Jews, Chinese, Japanese, Puerto Ricans, Portuguese, and others" (Cornell and Hartman 1998:6).

Another critique of Park's assimilation model was its inapplicability to the experiences of people racialized as racial minorities. In fact, E. Franklin Frazier, an African American doctoral student working with Park at Chicago, was the first to level this critique, arguing that Americans racialized as Black had still not been fully assimilated into American culture.

The path to assimilation for minorities racialized as Black has been blocked. Park (1950) acknowledged that the process might take longer for racial minorities, but he still argued that assimilation was inevitable. However, this remains a significant critique of Park's race relations cycle—that subordinate groups do not control the assimilationist process; dominant groups can and do block the assimilation of subordinate groups that they view as undesirable.

Another critique of the assimilationist paradigm popularized by Park is that he argued assimilation was not just inevitable but desirable. However, assimilation is not the only option for immigrant groups entering a new culture. Another option is **cultural pluralism**, the idea that groups can maintain ties to their culture of origin without threatening the dominant culture—that a society can be multiethnic/multicultural without it inevitably producing conflict. Many people in the United States, for instance, speak Spanish in their homes while still being fully functioning members of U.S. society, including speaking English in schools and in the workplace.

Another long-standing critique of the assimilationist paradigm is that it is an example of **Anglo-conformity** rather than a melting pot. The idea that immigrants came here from all over the world and melted into something new, the "American," is not exactly accurate. It is more accurate to say that immigrant groups come here and drop their cultural ties in favor of an Anglo, or White, culture. This distinction is important because it shows the advantages immigrants who come from English-speaking countries, as well as immigrants racialized as White, have over others (Gordon 1964; Sollors 2017).

Finally, while the race relations cycle was certainly evident in the observations Chicago School sociologists witnessed in their "laboratory" as they studied ethnic immigrant groups who were racialized as White in Chicago at the turn of the twentieth century, a major problem was Park's presumption that this pattern was generalizable to other groups, times, and places. He not only argued the "race relations cycle" could explain immigrant assimilation in Chicago at the turn of the century but argued that it was a universal phenomenon—that not only was the United States a "melting pot" but that the "melting pot" was global (Cornell and Hartmann 1998). Not only does this assimilationist perspective not hold true across cultures, but it does not even hold true for American society across time. For instance, German immigrants who came to the United States in the late 1840s sought to create little German communities. They established German-language newspapers, and public schools held classes in German rather than English because their goal was the preservation and cultivation of German culture. Essentially, they actively avoided assimilation (Cornell and Hartmann 1998). Despite Park's predictions of the demise of ethnicity in the U.S. and the globe, ethnicity remains a defining feature of individual identities as well as societies, which we explore in more detail later in this chapter.

Stages of Assimilation

In his book *Assimilation in American Life*, sociologist Milton Gordon (1964) expanded on Park's understanding of assimilation by theorizing assimilation as a seven-stage process, with each stage building upon the previous one. The first stage is **cultural assimilation** and refers to the early stage when immigrant groups begin to adopt the cultural patterns of the mainstream society. This stage is also referred to as **acculturation**, the process by which an individual adopts a new culture, changing one's behavior and attitudes to fit into one's new culture. The second stage of assimilation is **structural assimilation**, which refers to when an immigrant or minority group is absorbed into the mainstream society's associations and institutions—what Gordon (1984) called "cliques, clubs, and institutions." In other words, they can attend the same schools, be employed in the same establishments, and participate in the same social clubs as dominant-group members. Gordon felt this was an important stage of assimilation because it is within clubs and institutions that people from different groups can interact and get to know one another. Gordon's third stage is **marital assimilation**, which refers to when the immigrant or minority group has reached such a level of acceptance that intermarriage between the immigrant or minority group and the dominant group is acceptable (see Chapter 5).

Gordon's next stage is **identificational assimilation**, which is when the immigrant or minority group identifies with the mainstream, dominant group and no longer thinks of themselves as different. This stage has important political implications because the immigrant or minority group will no longer fight for their group's rights, since they view their rights as the same as those of the dominant group. The next stage, **attitude receptional assimilation**, is characterized by a lack of prejudice against the immigrant or minority group (see Chapter 3). The sixth stage Gordon identified is **behavior receptional assimilation**, which is characterized by lack of discrimination against the immigrant or minority group (see Chapter 4). The final stage of assimilation, according to Gordon's model, is **civic assimilation**, meaning the immigrant or minority group has become part of the dominant group such that there is no value or power conflict between the groups (Gordon, 1964). Gordon's stages of assimilation make it easier to see where the assimilation of racial minorities has been blocked in ways that European ethnic immigrants racialized as White have not.

Sociologist Alejandro Portes (1993) has challenged what is understood as the "straight line assimilationist" model associated with inevitable upward mobility with his notion of **segmented assimilation**, which recognizes three possible outcomes for the second generation other than inevitable, straight-line assimilation. Those are upward assimilation, downward assimilation, and upward mobility combined with bicultur-alism (Portes and Zhou 1993; Portes and Rumbaut 2001). These divergent paths are dependent upon the relations between immigrant children, their parents, and the wider ethnic community—specifically, whether these are consonant, dissonant, or a matter of selective acculturation. If the immigrant children and their parents engage in consonant acculturation, they learn American culture and abandon the ways of their culture of origin at roughly the same pace. These children are more likely to experience upward mobility because there is no tension between the parents and children in terms of cultural values; both embrace mainstream, American norms, and the immigrant child is encouraged to succeed in the U.S. according to U.S. standards, with the support of their parents. If the immigrant child and their parents experience dissonant acculturation, where the children adapt to American culture faster than their parents who resist cutting ties to their cultures of origin, the children are more likely to experience downward assimilation. According to Portes and Zhou (1993), **downward assimilation**, which refers to immigrants assimilating into impoverished groups, occurs when young immigrants are forced to confront American racism and limited economic opportunities while experiencing conflict with their parents' cultural values and a lack of ethnic community support. The third type, selective acculturation, is when both the immigrant children and their parents adapt to the mainstream, American culture and maintain close ties to their ethnic community. In this situation, parental authority remains and there is fluent bilingualism and little to no intergenerational conflict, all of which work to the advantage of the immigrants, particularly for those facing discrimination. Being able to rely on a community for support while learning a new culture holds tremendous value (Portes and Rumbaut 2001).

The importance of an ethnic community for immigrants has long been recognized as essential. Sociologists refer to these as **ethnic enclaves**, communities composed primarily of people from a particular immigrant group who live in close proximity to one another and offer employment opportunities for new arrivals and where there are ethnic businesses, such as groceries, restaurants, and shops that cater to the immigrant group's culture. Ethnic enclaves provide immigrants with a social buffer, a comfort zone in a strange new world. Most major urban areas in the U.S. have Chinatowns, which are a textbook example of an ethnic enclave. Chicago School sociologists recognized this need for immigrants to retain ties to their cultures of origin. They argued that "a premature severing of his [sic] ties to the past left the immigrant in a rootless and demoralized condition" (Persons 1987:53–54). However, immigrant groups today can have rich cultural ties with fellow immigrants, without living near them or necessarily being in a recognizable ethnic enclave.

More current scholars emphasize **neo-assimilation theory**, which resists the idea that immigrants must become similar to the dominant group, and instead they define assimilation as a decategorization process, where ethnic differences are of less interest to the dominant group and where assimilation is a two-way process, where both the dominant group and the immigrant group are changed by their encounter (Alba and Nee 2003).

The Continuing Significance of Ethnicity

Most social scientists who studied ethnicity followed the lead of Chicago School sociologists in predicting the inevitable assimilation of immigrants, to the point that they would drop their ancestral ties in the process of becoming an "American." By the 1970s, there was considerable evidence this was not happening. A different pattern was identified, that of an **ethnic revival**, the recognition that ethnic groups racialized as White, such as Irish Americans, German Americans, Italian Americans, and Polish Americans, were reclaiming and celebrating their ethnicity, countering a primary claim of the assimilationist paradigm. Ethnicity remains an important part of people's identities as the proliferation of hybrid identities makes clear—people who see themselves as Irish American, German American, Mexican American, Chinese American, and so forth. It also remains an important force for political mobilization. And yet, "it was not supposed to be this way. Ethnicity was expected to disappear as a force to be reckoned with in the 20th century" (Cornell and Hartmann 1998:4).

Historian Marcus Hansen (1938) was one of the earliest social scientists to recognize this phenomenon, recognizing that the grandchildren of immigrants were in a position of privilege that allowed them to reclaim their ethnicity. In other words, immigrants and their children focus on assimilating, fitting into American culture, while their grandchildren (the second-generation Americans) can comfortably embrace their ethnicity. Hanson (1996 [1938]:206) describes it as, "what the son wishes to forget, the grandson wishes to remember."

Sociologist Herbert Gans (1979) rejects the idea that there has been an ethnic revival and instead argues this is all evidence of a new stage of acculturation, one based upon identity and the "feeling of being Jewish or Italian" (Gans 1996:425). To capture this new dynamic, he introduced the idea of **symbolic ethnicity**, the embrace of one's ethnic heritage, particularly in the form of foods and festivals, such as Irish Americans celebrating St. Patrick's Day and Italian Americans celebrating St. Joseph's Day, as long as their embrace of their ethnic heritage does not challenge their middle-class, White American status. It is more of a leisure time activity. Other scholars refer to this as "dime store ethnicity," because

Irish dancing is a current example of symbolic ethnicity; a way for Irish Americans to connect with their Irish heritage in a way that does not threaten their White, middle-class American status.

people are choosing a grandparent to identify with while disregarding other ancestral lines, much the way one shops for products at a store (Stein and Hill 1977).

Other scholars pointed out that ethnicity also operated as a potent political mobilization tool. Racial and ethnic group members share fundamental political interests, and it is these interests that link them together as a collective, helping them maintain ties to their racial and ethnic groups (Glazer and Moynihan 1963). We see this today in the idea of **voting blocs**, groups of people who tend to vote in similar ways, in support of a political party or in support or opposition to particular social policies. People racialized as Black have been a solid Democratic voting bloc since the 1950s, for instance.

Sociologist Mary Waters (1990) studied the ongoing significance of ethnicity, specifically its salience for identity among third- and fourth-generation suburban White ethnics in the mid-1980s. She focused on sub-urban residents because these people lived outside the structural forces that helped maintain ethnicity—outside ethnic enclaves. Sociologists, she argues, have tended to "equate suburbanization and residential integration with assimilation" (Waters 1990:11). These are people who generally "fall off the sociologists' map" in terms of ethnicity.

Waters (1990) found that for ethnic Americans racialized as White, they have considerable choice in terms of their ethnic identification, including the option whether to ethnically identify at all and, if they choose to, which ethnicity to embrace. Ethnic identity for people racialized as White will not affect one's life much at all—as Waters (1990:147) states, "It does not, for the most part, limit choice of marriage partner . . . where you will live, who your friends will be, what job you will have, or whether you will be subject to discrimination. It matters only in voluntary ways—in celebrating holidays with a special twist, cooking a special ethnic meal." And yet, suburban ethnics racialized as White still cling to their ethnic identities and find it important to teach their children where they are from.

Racial/Ethnic Identity

People racialized as White, as noted previously, have choices in terms of their ethnicity, and countless scholars have explored this lingering presence of ethnicity among Americans racialized as White. However, people racialized as non-White are too often treated as if they are devoid of ethnicity (see Chapter 1). As Waters (1990:18) explains, "Whites enjoy a great deal of freedom in these [ethnic identity] choices, those defined in 'racial' terms as non-whites much less. Black Americans, for example, are highly constrained to identify as blacks, without other options available to them, even when they believe or know that their forebears included many non-blacks." Some scholars have explored reclamation of racial/ethnic identities among people racialized as non-White (Fitzgerald 2007; Nagel 1998; Rhea 1997). Research on Native American **reclaimers**, studies of people who either recently learned of or recently embraced their Native American ancestry to the point that it becomes a salient part of their identity, find that this process can help destabilize the racial hierarchy. When significant numbers of people who have White privilege reject their Whiteness and instead reclaim an identity racialized as non-White, it diminishes the power of the racial hierarchy (Fitzgerald 2007). Other scholars have explored the changing racial identities among biracial and multiracial people (Korgen 1998; Rockquemore and Brunsma 2002). In the post–civil rights era, the embrace of a biracial or multiracial identity has become an option for people in ways it was not for previous generations (see Chapter 5).

The Racialization of Immigrants
••

While historically much more attention has been paid to immigrants racialized as White in both social science research and in the U.S. national narrative, in the current era, the **racialization of immigrants** takes prominence, where our perception of immigrants shifts from understanding them as ethnic to understanding them as racialized as non-White, and hostility and anti-immigrant sentiment accompany this shift (Sáenz and Douglas 2015). The current racialization of immigrants has primarily targeted immigrants from Central and South America and those from the Middle East.

This should not imply that the racialization of immigrants in the U.S. is a new phenomenon. Indeed, there is a long history of racializing immigration, despite our national narrative that portrays the United States as welcoming, challenging the Emma Lazarus poem at the foot of the Statue of Liberty claiming, "Give me your tired, your poor/Your huddled masses, yearning to breathe free." For instance, immigration restrictions have always been about the exclusion of people perceived as incapable of assimilating, people racialized as Other. The first immigration restrictions were implemented in 1875 with the passage of the Page Law, which restricted Chinese women from legally entering the U.S. This was a strategy designed to keep Chinese men from being able to stay in the U.S. The period from the 1850s to 1880s witnessed high Chinese immigration, mostly in California and on the West Coast. Chinese laborers were essential to mining, agriculture, and building the transcontinental railroad. Despite their important contributions, they faced intense hostility, were viewed as incapable of assimilating into American society, and were perceived as diseased (see Chapter 3). The Page Law restricted Chinese men's abilities to bring their families with them, while antimiscegenation laws limited their ability to marry Whites (see Chapter 5). If they were incapable of forming families or bringing their families with them when they came here for work, it was hoped they would eventually return to China and not try to become American.

By 1882, the federal government passed the Chinese Exclusion Act, which not only restricted most Chinese from immigrating to the U.S. but also made it impossible for those already here to become citizens. This legislation was repeatedly renewed, until the passage of the National Origins Act in 1924, which limited Asian immigration more broadly and showed favoritism toward immigrants from Europe. This legislation remained in place until 1965, when the Hart-Celler Act, otherwise known as the Immigration and Nationality Act, passed. This legislation abolished the national origins quotas and made family unification a priority. This legislation has literally changed the face of America because it opened the doors to immigrants from Asia, the Caribbean, and Latin America, who had mostly been barred under the National Origins Act.

In the current era, states have attempted to pass anti-immigrant legislation. While this type of legislation has only partially survived court challenges, since only the federal government has the right to legislate immigration, the fact that states are attempting to do so is evidence of the current climate of **xenophobia**, a term that refers to the fear and hatred of strangers and characterizes anti-immigrant environments. Arizona's SB

1070, discussed in Chapter 4, is one example of such legislation. Under this law, police officers have the right to check a person's immigration status if they are suspicious. This kind of policy is clearly racialized because immigrants racialized as White will not come under police officer suspicion in the way those racialized as Black or Brown will. Arizona passed SB 1070 in 2010, and soon after, Georgia, Utah, Indiana, South Carolina, and Alabama passed similar laws. Most have been blocked by the courts.

More evidence of the xenophobia of the modern era includes record immigrant deportations under the Obama administration and the criminalization of immigrants (see Chapter 4). However, nothing comes close to the xenophobia of President Trump's campaign rhetoric and his administration's actions. From his promise of a border wall along the U.S.–Mexico border, to his vilification of immigrants as criminals, his executive order to fund the construction of more immigrant detention facilities, family separation policies, and the over 2,300 traumatized migrant children warehoused in cages, the vilification and criminalization of immigrants is in full effect (Vinson 2020). The Trump administration has implemented a zero-tolerance policy on immigration where "everyone crossing the border—even those seeking asylum—were treated like a criminal. The government took away their children . . . and failed to create a reunification system, leaving parents unable to reunite with—or even track—their children" (Vinson 2020).

Under President Trump, xenophobic attitudes have increased, including family separation policies. As of October 2020, it was announced that 545 migrant children who had been separated from their parents at the border are missing.

Birthright Citizenship and Race

In the current era, much anti-immigrant hostility is linked to **birthright citizenship**, the part of the 14th Amendment (1868) that declared that any child born on U.S. soil is a U.S. citizen. Those who oppose birthright citizenship claim that it sets the United States up to be exploited through pregnant women coming here to have their children, a practice sometimes referred to as "birth tourism." These children are referred to as "anchor babies" because their citizenship is perceived as increasing the parent's chances of gaining permanent residency and U.S. citizenship. Opponents want to change the Constitution to say that at least one of the parents must be a naturalized citizen for birthright citizenship to be valid. In October of 2018, President Trump announced he was going to issue an executive order to overturn birthright citizenship; he would "instruct federal authorities to refuse to recognize the citizenship of children born in the United States if their parents are not citizens" (Epps 2018). He has yet to do so. But if he does take this action, the consequences would be dire; it would "create a shadow population of American-born people who have no state, no legal protection, and no real rights that the government is bound to respect" (Epps 2018).

Since birthright citizenship emerged with the passage of the 14th Amendment, the idea has long been wedded to race. During the early 1800s, the question of citizenship for free people racialized as Black was hotly contested (Jones 2018). The Supreme Court case *Dred Scott v. Sandford* (1857) intended to resolve the issue by declaring that people racialized as Black could never become citizens because of their race. In that case, Chief Justice Roger B. Taney infamously wrote that people racialized as Black "had no rights which the white man was bound to respect." This decision was highly controversial at the time in free states. The outcome of the Civil War and the passage of the 14th Amendment in 1868 overturned the *Dred Scott* decision.

Toward a More Racially Just Society

Moving toward a more racially just society must include a shift away from the xenophobic attitudes and policies of the current era and toward the humanization of immigrants. Humanizing immigrants begins with our language because "it conditions people who hear it to look the other way when those who are described in less-than-human ways suffer, or worse, to directly contribute to injustices themselves" (Kapitan 2019). One example of dehumanizing language is routinely referring to undocumented immigrants as "illegals" and "illegal aliens." In 2018, the Department of Justice even instructed U.S. attorneys to use the words "illegal alien" instead of "undocumented immigrant" (Kapitan 2019). The racial justice organization Race Forward initiated the Campaign to Eliminate the I-Word, "illegal," in 2010, operating on the assumption that no human is illegal. Using the language of our country as "overrun" or that we are victimized by an "invasion" of illegal aliens justifies the criminalization of immigrants and the increased militarization of the border (Kapitan 2019). More specifically, in the face of COVID-19, one step toward racial justice would be to release the tens of thousands of immigrants crowded in detention facilities and at extremely high risk of contracting the novel coronavirus.

In addition to humanizing immigrants, the path to racial justice also includes a **deracialization** process, which refers to eradicating the racial hierarchy (Stevens 2014). This is different from committing to colorblindness, which some might see as eliminating racial difference. As described in Chapter 1, racial differences are not the problem; the racial hierarchy, the fact that one group is advantaged based upon phenotype while others are disadvantaged, is the problem.

Conclusion
••

This chapter investigates the distinction between race and ethnicity, the disproportionate attention sociologists have paid to ethnicity at the expense of race, and the lingering presence of ethnicity, despite scholars' claims it would recede in importance over the generations. We then explore the assimilationist paradigm, its limitations and current adaptations in terms of segmented assimilation and neo-assimilation theory. The chapter then shifts to an exploration of the racialization of immigrants, both historically and currently, ending with a call to humanize immigrants as part of the path to a more racially just society.

KEY TERMS AND CONCEPTS ————————

Acculturation   30
Anglo-conformity   29
Assimilationism   27

Attitude receptional assimilation   30
Behavior receptional
   assimilation   30

CRITICAL THINKING QUESTIONS

1. Ask your parents and/or grandparents what is known about your family history. Are any of your ancestors immigrants? If so, what do you know about their assimilation, if anything? How does the melting pot narrative exclude some Americans? Why does this matter? Is your family history closer to traditional understandings of assimilation presented by Park and Gordon or closer to the segmented assimilation model introduced by Portes?

2. When did you learn the national narrative of the U.S. as a melting pot, if at all? When did you first learn information that challenged that narrative, if you learned it initially? If you were educated outside the United States, what did you learn about the U.S. and immigration, if anything? Provide evidence of the current racialization of immigrants.

RECOMMENDED READING

Cornell, Stephen and Douglas Hartmann. 1998. *Ethnicity and Race: Making Identities in a Changing World*. Thousand Oaks, CA: Pine Forge Press.

Gordon, Milton. 1964. *Assimilation in American Life*. New York: Oxford University Press.

Jones, Martha S. 2018. *Birthright Citizens: A History of Race and Rights in Antebellum America*. Cambridge, UK: Cambridge University Press.

Takaki, Ronald. 1990. *Iron Cages: Race and Culture in 19th Century America*. New York: Oxford University Press.

Takaki, Ronald. 1993. *A Different Mirror: A History of Multicultural America*. Boston, MA: Little, Brown and Company.

Waters, Mary. 1990. *Ethnic Options: Choosing Identities in America*. Berkeley, CA: University of California Press.

NOTE

1. Scholar Aldon D. Morris (2015) convincingly challenges the origin story of American sociology that has the University of Chicago as the birthplace. He argues in *The Scholar Denied* that the true origins of the discipline of sociology in the United States were at Atlanta University, a historically Black college or university, under the leadership of W. E. B. DuBois. In other words, "The first school of scientific sociology in the United States was founded by a black professor located in a historically black university in the South" (Morris 2015:1).

CHAPTER 3

Prejudice and Stereotyping

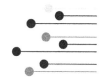

In Chapter 1, we defined racism, and part of that definition referred to "the implicit beliefs and acts that justify the assertion of power" (Magee 2019:14). This chapter is going to focus on the "beliefs" noted in that definition—a specific aspect of racism referred to as prejudice. **Prejudice** is racism manifesting in the form of attitudes—specifically, the preconceived attitudes or opinions, generally negative, about a group of people that are resistant to change, even in the face of contradictory evidence. If a person believes that people racialized as Latinx are lazy and, thus, undesirable as employees or coworkers, this is an example of racial prejudice; it is a negative attitude the person holds about a group of people. The person who believes people racialized as Latinx are lazy can still hold this racial prejudice even if they work with a person racialized as Latinx who defies that characterization and is a hard worker. That is a key aspect of prejudice: the tendency not to change one's opinion even in the face of contradictory evidence. In this situation, instead of the presence of the hardworking coworker racialized as Latinx dislodging the negative stereotypes about workers racialized as Latinx, the person instead decides that their coworker is an exception to the rule. In this respect, prejudice is quite irrational.

Despite the appearance of irrationality, social psychologists argue that prejudice is not only common, but normal (Allport 1954). At its core is the idea that human beings are social creatures, and as such, we form groups based upon all kinds of criteria, including racial group membership, and that we have a tendency toward **ethnocentrism**, the belief that our group's ways are correct, normal, and even superior to the ways of other groups. A certain amount of ethnocentrism is normal, and prejudice is at least partially an extension of that. As social psychologist Gordon W. Allport (1954:47) explains, "In-group loyalty does not necessarily imply hostility toward out-groups." However, both ethnocentrism and prejudice, when taken to the extreme, can be dangerous and manifest well beyond normal in-group favoritism to hostility and even violence toward out-groups.

While we often perceive attitudes as something held by individuals, they are also cultural, created and perpetuated through socialization, interactions, and especially through the media. In other words, we learn the racial prejudices that are dominant in our culture. We do not have to agree with them, but we usually know the dominant racial prejudices that exist in our culture because they are pervasive—repeated in films, television, advertising, common jokes, and the framing of news stories, just to name a few.

Attitude–Behavior Connections

To what extent does holding negative racial attitudes about a group or groups result in discrimination, acting on those prejudices? There is no clear relationship between attitudes and behaviors; we cannot assume that people who hold racial prejudice will discriminate, nor can we assume that discrimination is the result of racial prejudice. Work by sociologist Robert Merton (1976) showing the ways prejudice and discrimination can vary helps clarify the attitude–behavior connection. Merton identified four categories to capture this variance: the unprejudiced nondiscriminator, the unprejudiced discriminator, the prejudiced nondiscriminator, and the prejudiced discriminator. According to Merton, unprejudiced nondiscriminators, also known as all-weather liberals in his schema, are people who do not hold racial prejudices and do not discriminate. Their attitudes and behaviors are consistent, predictable, and unsurprising. The second category, unprejudiced discriminators, also known as fair-weather liberals, might be more surprising. Why would someone who does not hold racial prejudice actively discriminate? For any number of reasons, this might happen. For instance, a restaurant manager who does not view herself as racially prejudiced but who manages a restaurant in a section of a city that is well known for its racial prejudice may not hire people racialized as non-White for waitress and bartender positions because they would not be well received by the restaurant's clientele. This could result in the employee being discriminated against by customers in terms of verbal harassment or poor tips, or fewer customers patronizing the restaurant because they do not want to be waited on by a person racialized as non-White, negatively impacting the business. A fair-weather liberal's actions are inconsistent with their beliefs, but they feel pressure to discriminate, instead of adhering to their personal value system. People who fall into the third category, which Merton referred to as the timid bigot or the prejudiced nondiscriminator, also have inconsistent attitudes and beliefs. These are people who hold racial prejudices but do not act on them because of laws or social norms that make discriminating costly for them. If a restaurant manager held racial prejudices, they may personally prefer to only hire people racialized as Black or Brown for the less lucrative "back of the house" positions. However, when confronted with perfectly qualified minority applicants, a corporate atmosphere that embraces diversity, and civil rights laws that make it illegal to discriminate, they may not act on their prejudice and, instead, hire the person racialized as non-White for the "front of the house" position. Merton's final group, the prejudiced discriminators, also referred to as active bigots, have consistent attitudes and beliefs; they hold racial prejudices and act on them, discriminating against racial minorities when they can. This final category is, like the first one, unsurprising.

As Merton's typology on prejudice and discrimination reveals, social context matters. While one cannot pass a law that makes a person's beliefs illegal, we can and have made acting on some beliefs illegal. When it is illegal to discriminate, a person who holds racial prejudice may think twice about acting on that prejudice, as the timid bigot exemplifies. While Merton's typology makes a certain amount of sense, we do see that racial prejudice can be an influence in other ways, such as through support or opposition to social policies and through the manifestation of prejudice as stereotypes in the media, both discussed later.

Manifestations of Prejudice

Scholarship on racism was centered on the psychology of prejudice, or the ways prejudice manifests in individuals, for decades. There is a large body of research on prejudice and bias, the role of racism in public opinion, and on eradicating prejudice, with social psychologist Gordon W. Allport's (1954) *The Nature of Prejudice* regarded as the foundational work in this area. In this work, Allport explored the history of prejudice, its effect on victims, and ways to reduce prejudice. He introduced the **intergroup contact hypothesis**, which argued that prejudice could be reduced through intergroup contact as long as the following conditions were met: the groups had equal status, there was a common goal, there was cooperation, and there was support of authorities, law, or custom. Team sports are an example of the kind of intergroup contact where these criteria are met.

Much of the current work in the field is focused on aversive racism and White racial resentment, discussed later. Most sociological research on racism has shifted from a focus on individual prejudice and discrimination toward institutional racism (see Chapter 4). The research on prejudice shifted as well to focusing on the expression of racism in the perceptions that racial minorities "do not abide by the norms of hard work and patriotism." (Cramer 2019:154). In other words, in the current era, a person who holds racial prejudices is less likely to think "I don't like Black people" and more likely to think, "I don't understand. Why won't Black people just take any job?"

Research has consistently found that racial prejudice has declined in the 50 years since the civil rights movement (Devine and Elliot 1996; Gaertner and Dovidio 1986; Madon et al. 2001; Pearson, Dovidio, and Gaertner 2009; Schuman, Steeh, Bobo, and Kryson 1997). Despite these research findings, questions remain. Are people less prejudiced today, or are they simply uncomfortable acknowledging their racism in the current era? The answer is unclear. The United States proclaims a commitment to egalitarian values, which are almost universally supported; thus, racial prejudice is no longer as acceptable as it was in previous eras. Yet racial prejudice remains and currently is better captured by the term **aversive racism**, which refers to a contemporary type of racism that operates unconsciously in people who regard themselves as unprejudiced, even though they hold negative views of members of minority groups. The term was originally used to describe educated White liberals but is more widely applied to any dominant-group member (Dovidio and Gaertner 2007). An aversive racist will "sympathize with victims of past injustice, support principles of racial equality, and genuinely regard themselves as non-prejudiced, but at the same time possess conflicting and often non-conscious, negative feelings and beliefs about Blacks that are rooted in basic psychological processes that promote racial bias" (Pearson, Dovidio, and Gaertner 2009:316).

Some research finds White opposition to social policies that are perceived to be race-conscious, such as affirmative action, is based in racial prejudice. This dynamic is referred to as **White racial resentment**— "the belief that African Americans should not get, and do not deserve assistance from the government to overcome their social and economic position" (Mangun and DeHaan 2019:422). People racialized as Black and Brown face disproportionate poverty rates and unemployment that have resulted in the implementation of some social policies to address their disadvantaged economic position (see Chapter 4). This is what inspires White racial resentment—the idea that people racialized as White are making it on their own, without government assistance, while people racialized as non-White are relying on government handouts. What is overlooked by this argument is that people racialized as White have long been recipients of social policies that were denied to people racialized as African American, such as Social Security, the GI Bill, and government-backed federal housing loans and that more people racialized as White rely on government assistance programs that people racialized as minorities are perceived to be exploiting, such as TANF (Temporary Aid for Needy Families, colloquially known as welfare) (Katznelson 2005; Oliver and Shapiro 1995; Quadagno 1994; Williams 2003). Additionally, the perception of affirmative action as a race-conscious policy itself is a misunderstanding; it is a policy that is designed to provide women and people racialized as non-White opportunities that were previously closed off to them, and in fact, women racialized as White have benefited more than any other marginalized group from affirmative action. Despite this, it is rarely referred to as a gender-conscious policy.

Research on racial resentment finds that people racialized as White are more likely to disapprove of policies they perceive as benefitting people racialized as minorities. This image is of protesters who were against passage of the Affordable Care Act, colloquially known as "Obamacare."

There is a considerable amount of research on racial resentment, including its influence on attitudes toward welfare policies (Feldman and Huddy 2005; Wetts and Willer 2018), attitudes toward affirmative action (Mangum and DeHaan 2016), evaluations of former first lady Michelle Obama (Knuckey and Myunghee 2016), use of firearms (Filindra and Kaplan 2017), and support for policies that benefit wealthy people and corporations, while having detrimental effects on the health and life expectancy of working-class and poor people racialized as White (Metzl 2019).

Scholars have designed a standard racial resentment scale asking respondents whether they agree or disagree with—and how strongly they agree or disagree with—the following statements:

- Irish, Italian, Jewish, and many other minorities overcame prejudice and worked their way up. Blacks should do the same without any special favors.

- Generations of slavery and discrimination have created conditions that make it difficult for Blacks to work their way out of their lower class.

- Over the past few years, Blacks have gotten less than they deserve.

- It's really a matter of some people just not trying hard enough: if Blacks would only try harder, they could be just as well off as Whites (Cramer 2020; Kinder and Sanders 1996).

The consistent use of this scale in research over the last 25 years helps us to understand the role of White racial resentment in "public opinion in the era of the first black president, Obama, and the racially inflammatory rhetoric of the Trump campaign and administration" (Cramer 2020:155).

Another line of scholarship on the manifestations of prejudice has been based in perceptions of racial group competition. Initial work in this area was by Herbert Blumer (1958), who argued that racial prejudice emerges when the dominant group feels their dominance, or their group position, is being threatened. Specifically, "out-group hostility was a product of individuals' desire to preserve a superior status for their in-group. When they perceive that a salient out-group threatens this status, hostility emerges" (Cramer 2020:155). The election of Barack Obama to the presidency was interpreted by many people racialized as White as a threat to their dominant-group status, even though people racialized as White disproportionately held political power then and since. After the election, people racialized as White declared the country to be postracial (Fitzgerald 2014). A postracial society would be one where people racialized as White were no longer dominant, the ultimate threat to group position. Of course, there is no validity to the claim that the U.S. was or is postracial, but Blumer's theory is based upon a group member's perception of their group's status.

Sociologist Lawrence Bobo and colleagues extended Blumer's understanding of racism and group position and the idea of prejudice as emerging from racial group competition in the current era in more depth, paying specific attention to the way this dynamic plays out in a multiracial society (Bobo and Hutchings 1996). For instance, they find "substantial percentages (though typically less than 50 percent), of Whites, Blacks, Latinos, and Asians perceive members of other groups as zero-sum competitive threats for social resources" (Bobo and Hutchings 1996:966). These findings show that the more a group racialized as minority feels collectively oppressed, the more likely they are to perceive out-groups as a threat.

Stereotypes

One of the primary ways prejudice manifests is through stereotypes. **Stereotypes** refer to exaggerated or oversimplified portrayals of a group of people (Fitzgerald 2017b). Another way to think about this is that stereotypes "refer to the typical picture that comes to mind when thinking about a particular social group" (Dovidio, Hewstone, Glick, and Esses 2010:7). Stereotypes can be positive or negative, but they ultimately act as shorthand, allowing people to assume they know something about an individual due to their race. All groups hold stereotypes about out-groups; while people racialized as White hold stereotypes about people racialized as Black, people racialized as Black also hold stereotypes about people racialized as White. However, because people racialized as White are the sociological and statistical majority (see Chapter 1) and still hold most of the power in society, the stereotypes they hold are more likely to be perpetuated in the media, frame how teachers perceive students, and influence considerations such as who is a better employee, who is defined as deviant or criminally inclined, and so on.

We all learn the dominant racial stereotypes in our culture through **socialization**, a term that refers to how we learn, through interaction with others, that which we must know in order to survive and thrive in our culture. This is why often even people racialized as non-White have internalized dominant-group stereotypes of their group, a phenomena known as **internalized racism**; "most of us have internalized the messages of our culture that reward us for biases *against* brown and black people, and reward us for biases *in favor of* whites" (Magee 2019:77). An important thing to keep in mind about stereotypes is that they function to justify racial inequality and the status quo; they help to make it seem normal and natural. We are going to explore the primary stereotypes surrounding racial minorities in the U.S., keeping in mind how such stereotypes can result in discrimination and racial inequality (see Chapter 4).

Stereotypes of Asian Americans

A common stereotype associated with people racialized as Asian American is that of the **model minority**, the idea that people racialized as Asian American succeed in ways other immigrant groups do not, making them ideal minorities. The term was originally coined in 1966 to describe the Japanese American experience and reemerged in the 1980s during the Reagan administration (Kitano and Daniels 2001; Thakore 2016). Collectively, people racialized as Asian American do have higher rates of success on most socioeconomic measures, particularly income, home ownership, and educational attainment. Even a positive stereotype like this is problematic because emphasizing the ways many people racialized as Asian American have succeeded masks the racial discrimination that they face. The dominant group created this stereotype to claim that the American dream is attainable for immigrants and People of Color, even though immigrants and people racialized as racial minorities are less likely to attain it. The stereotype of the model minority also emerged at a time when social welfare programs were increasingly under attack, so the concept was used to dispel the claim that racism was the cause of racial inequality (Chou and Feagin 2008). It is meant to downplay societal racism overall while also softening the racism that people racialized as Asian American experience.

The model minority stereotype is also problematic because "Asian American" is an umbrella term that homogenizes the vastly different experiences of numerous groups of people. While people racialized as Asian American collectively do well on most measures of socioeconomic success, some of them face considerable disadvantage, which the model minority stereotype obscures. A final critique of the model minority stereotype is that for people racialized as Asian American, their success on measures like socioeconomic status and educational attainment should make them model citizens, not model minorities.

An extension of this model minority stereotype of people racialized as Asian American is the perception of them as academically excellent, as evidenced by their group scores on standardized tests and their superior college preparedness and motivation. These positive stereotypes come at a price, though, as they are also portrayed as "robotic overachievers in the classroom who are nerdy, passive, or inept on a social level" (Chou and Feagin 2008:55). This stereotype is problematic on several levels. First, not all people racialized as Asian American are academically gifted, but even most teachers operate on the assumption they are, which means many students racialized as Asian American who need help are not getting it (Hartlep 2013; Lee 2009; Lew 2003; Teranishi 2010). Academic success among people racialized as Asian American varies not only individually; as scholar Nicholas Daniel Hartlep (2013:ix) explains, there are "huge gaps within Asian American subgroups in academic achievement levels." Second, the academic success of students racialized as Asian American in schools can make the racism they experience less visible. For instance, children racialized as Asian American face racist taunting throughout their school years, and teachers and administrators fail to reprimand students for the teasing. In predominantly White schools, sports programs, student government, and many school organizations are **White spaces**, spaces where people racialized as non-White feel unwelcome and are treated as intruders while students racialized as White feel a sense of belonging, limiting the participation of students racialized as non-White (Moore 2008; Chou and Feagin 2008).

Stereotypes of people racialized as non-White are designed to convince others of their inferiority and deviance, so it is unsurprising that racial stereotypes are also sexualized. Stereotypes of men racialized as Asian American, for instance, portray them as effeminate, emasculated, and hyposexual. Women racialized as Asian American have been fetishized; stereotypes of women racialized as Asian American portray them as both passive and sexually exotic, seductive yet untrustworthy (Chou 2012).

Another stereotype targeting people racialized as Asian and Asian American resurfaced recently in the face of the COVID-19 pandemic: that of Asians representing a "yellow peril." The stereotype has resurfaced several times over the years: first, in the late nineteenth century in response to high Chinese immigration; second, in response to the Cold War and the fear of Communism; and today, in the form of violent attacks against people who are racialized as Asian American who are being scapegoated for the emergence of the novel coronavirus. Fox News personality Tucker Carlson, President Trump, and some Republican representatives, such as Kevin McCarthy, have, for instance, referred to the disease as the "Chinese coronavirus" and "kung flu" despite the fact that the World Health Organization issued protocols for naming new diseases in 2015 that specifically stated that geographic locations, animals, and groups of people should be avoided in the naming (Pygas 2020). Early in the spread of the pandemic in the United States and before the shutdown, Chinese restaurants were empty, flights to China were canceled as travel restrictions were implemented, and people racialized as Asian American faced increased harassment, discrimination, and violence due to the pandemic (Lee 2020). In one of dozens of similar stories, a man racialized as Asian American was attacked on the Upper East Side of Manhattan on March 10, 2020. The 59-year-old man was kicked to the ground and injured by a teenager yelling, "F—ing Chinese coronavirus!" This was the second such attack on a person racialized as Asian American that day in New York (Moore 2020). Schoolchildren racialized as Asian American are also being targeted for racial harassment, with some being called "corona" (Escobar 2020).

The stereotype of people racialized as Asian as a "yellow peril" and as pollutants has a long history (Lee 1999). In the late nineteenth and early twentieth centuries, people racialized as Asian, the so-called "yellow race," were perceived as a threat to the Western world and to White supremacy (Chou and Feagin 2015; Kawai 2005; Lee 1999; Nguyen, Carter, and Cater 2019; Okihiro 1994). Partially fueled by a dramatic increase in Chinese immigration in the late 1800s, the stereotype of them as a "yellow peril" saturated the media. They were portrayed as deviant, villainous, dangerous, and disease-ridden invaders (Del Visco 2019). Like the scapegoating of Jews for the bubonic plague in the 1300s, Irish immigrants for the typhoid epidemic in the 1800s, Haitian Americans and gay men for HIV in the 1980s, and West Africans for Ebola in 2014, Asian Americans are being targeted today for the COVID-19 pandemic.

> During disease outbreaks, attacks on marginalized groups
> are not an exception, but the norm. Racism and xenophobia
> are additionally stoked by discourse that casts the bodies and
> behaviors of Chinese Americans and other Asian Americans as

THE ONLY ONE BARRED OUT.

ENLIGHTENED AMERICAN STATESMAN.—" We must draw the line *somewhere*, you know."

This cartoon shows the hypocrisy of the United States, celebrated for its embrace of immigrants, and the arbitrariness of the banning of Chinese immigrants by the Chinese Exclusion Act.

suspicious and even at fault for spreading disease. While viruses and other pathogens do not discriminate between hosts based on race, ethnicity, nationality or immigration status—stigma and misinformation certainly do. (Lee 2020)

For people racialized as Asian American, the revival of the "yellow peril" stereotype symbolizes their precariousness as Americans and their status as perpetual foreigners. From the earliest hostility to Chinese immigrants, the most common reaction was that they would never be able to assimilate into American society. During the pandemic, when a food sample vendor at a Costco told a Korean American woman and her children to get away from the samples, asking if they had just come from China, the woman's spouse said, "It just reminds me that when people look at us, they don't see an American" (Escobar 2020).

Stereotypes of Black Americans

Many of the anti-Black stereotypes that circulate today are updated versions of anti-Black stereotypes that emerged to justify the violence of slavery and Jim Crow. These stereotypes were initially perpetuated through minstrel shows (the most popular form of entertainment between the 1830s and 1910), songs, newspaper cartoons, educational materials, and eventually television and film, among other sources. There are a handful of stereotypes of men racialized as Black portraying them as docile, simple-minded, sometimes musical, lazy, and childlike, from the "Sambo," to "Uncle Tom," to "coons," or the "musical old darky"; these stereotypes sent the message that men racialized as Black not only belonged in servitude but they were actually content as slaves (Bolge 1994; Boskin 1986). Some of the earliest stereotypes of women racialized as Black include the mammy, who was a passive servant, completely devoted to her master and his family, and the hypersexual jezebel, a stereotype that was intended to shift blame from men racialized as White for the rape of women racialized as Black onto the women racialized as Black themselves, as if they were seducing the men rather than rape victims (Goings 1997; Collins 1990).

During the Jim Crow era, a new stereotype of men racialized as Black emerged: that of the savage, violent brute with a sexual appetite for women racialized as White. This stereotype justified the lynching of thousands of men racialized as Black throughout the South. The dominant stereotypes of men racialized as African American remain that they are violent and hypersexual, which results in their increased likelihood of being policed through racial profiling (see Chapter 4). We can see the influence of the stereotype of men racialized as Black as lazy in attitudes toward social policies by people racialized as White: "Whites who believe that they are much more hard-working than African Americans, Hispanics, and Asian Americans are more likely to think that affirmative action is a bad thing while Whites who do not believe they are much more hardworking than African Americans, Hispanics, and Asian Americans are more likely to think that affirmative action is a good thing" (Mangum and DeHaan 2019:432).

The same logic can be applied to the most common stereotype of women racialized as Black today: that of a welfare mother, unwilling to work and willing to let the state support her as she recklessly has more children (Collins 1990; Hurwitz, Peffley, and Sniderman 1997). The stereotype of the Black welfare mother highlights her supposed low morals and deviant sexual appetite. This stereotype results in White opposition to welfare, formally called Temporary Aid for Needy Families (TANF), even though more women racialized as White are on welfare than are women racialized as Black. Sociologist Patricia Hill Collins (1990) refers to such racial

This image of two Black women and multiple children implies the widespread stereotype that Black women are deviant and recklessly have children they cannot afford, thus relying on welfare to support them. The reality is that most welfare recipients are White.

stereotypes perpetuated through media as **controlling images** because they serve to justify racism, sexism, and poverty and make them appear normal and natural; thus, these racial stereotypes are a form of social control.

As with the discussion of stereotypes about people racialized as Asian American, some stereotypes about people racialized as African American appear positive yet are still problematic. One of those stereotypes pertains to the perception of superior athleticism of people racialized as Black. Anthropologist Earnest Hooton was one of the first people to promote stereotypes about both Black criminality and Black athleticism in the 1920s. While his work was criticized by fellow scientists at the time, these kinds of stereotypes remain. The stereotype of the "natural Black athlete" is pervasive (Azzarito and Harrison 2008). Once again, while positive, there are drawbacks to even positive stereotypes. First, we find this pervasive in sports announcers' rhetoric—they present athletes racialized as Black as natural athletes while pushing a narrative that professional athletes racialized as White got where they are through hard work. Any elite, professional athlete got where they are through years of hard work. While of course some people are born with more natural athletic abilities than others, one cannot make it to the level of elite athlete on natural talent alone. A second problem with this stereotype is that it is used to fuel a "Black brawn versus White brain" stereotype; the idea that if people racialized as Black are exceptional athletes, it comes at the expense of their intellectual capabilities. This manifests even in higher education, where students racialized as Black on campus are presumed to be athletes and not academically inclined students who earned their acceptance the same way their classmates did: through hard work, a history of academic achievement, and a little bit of luck.

Stereotypes of Latinxs

According to scholar Charles Ramírez Berg (2002), there are six stereotypes of people racialized as Latinxs that have dominated Hollywood film, and by extension U.S. culture, for over 100 years: the bandito, or criminal; the male buffoon; the Latin lover; the harlot; the female clown; and the dark lady. Like the most prominent stereotypes of people racialized as African American, these racial stereotypes are linked to criminality and deviance (the bandito and the dark lady), deviant hypersexuality (the Latin lover and the harlot), and clownish/foolish characters (the male and female buffoons). You might be more familiar with the current manifestations of these in Hollywood films and television as the Latinx maid, the hypersexualized, "spicy" Latinx, or the drug pusher/kingpin/gangbanging Latinx (Anderson 2017). According to USC's Annenberg Inclusion Initiative, a qualitative analysis of 200 top films between 2017 and 2018 found that 24 percent of Latinx characters were criminals, with 61.9 percent of those engaged in gangs, drug dealing, or organized crime (Smith et al. 2019). With the pervasiveness of the Latinx criminal stereotype, it is no surprise that when

President Trump kicked off his campaign with the announcement that Mexican immigrants were rapists and drug dealers, he found some traction with voters. Research by USC's Annenberg School also found that people racialized as Latinx, who were 18.1 percent of the U.S. population in 2017, were seriously underrepresented in content creator roles behind the camera, such as producers, writers, and directors, in addition to being underrepresented in leading roles in front of the camera, so the perpetuation of stereotypes in film and television is unsurprising (Smith et al. 2019).

Stereotypes of Native Americans

Like the stereotypes of men racialized as Black, stereotypes of men racialized as Native American focus on their presumably violent nature. One of the oldest stereotypes of people racialized as Native American is that they are violent "savages" while people racialized as White are innocent victims of their savagery (Hirschfelder and Molder 2018). Long-standing stereotypes of women racialized as Native American portray them as sexually promiscuous and as a threat to women racialized as White and their families (D'Emilio and Freedman 2012).

Research by Virginia McLaurin (2019) that looked at 60 TV shows, films, and books from the early 1990s to 2011 found that very little had changed in terms of the stereotyping of people racialized as Native American. In her contemporary analysis, she found that people racialized as Native American fell into two categories, "good" and "bad" Indians, which paralleled old stereotypes of the "noble savage" and the "savage." In the past, a "good" Indian helped Europeans while the "bad" Indian was uncooperative and resisted European encroachment. Today, media portrayals of "good" Indians show them as impoverished, living on reservations, and culturally knowledgeable compared to the "bad" Indians who are out of touch with their cultures, even to the point of being inauthentically Native, receiving government benefits, untrustworthy, and often run casinos. As McLaurin (2019) explains, "the implication being that 'real' indigenous people are impoverished, helpful to outsiders, and totally immersed in traditional indigenous culture."

Ethnic Stereotypes

This chapter has explored the most prominent racial stereotypes in the United States. There are also ethnic stereotypes targeting Jewish, Arab, and Irish Americans, among others, that proliferate in our culture. Stereotypes of the Irish as violent, criminally inclined, and lacking morals were dominant in the mid-to-late 1800s, emerging in response to rising rates of Irish immigration. Much like stage and film characterizations of people racialized as Black, stereotypes of Irish Americans on stage included stock characters such as the "Jim Dandy, the drunken, belligerent, and foolish Pat and Bridget" (Ignatiev 1995:2). A long-standing antisemitic stereotype is of Jews as disloyal to the U.S. and instead as loyal to Israel. Additionally, Jewish stereotypes include the idea that they hold too much power in the business world and engage in unethical business practices ("Anti-Semitic Stereotypes" 2020). Stereotypes of Arabs and Arab Americans have long portrayed them as barbaric, greedy, and untrustworthy and, currently, as terrorists (Selod 2018; Shaheen 2014). Muslim women, especially those who wear the hijab, are stereotyped as oppressed, weak, and antifeminist (Selod 2018). These are just a few examples; stereotyping of racial/ethnic others is pervasive in our culture.

Toward a More Racially Just Society

Previously, we introduced Gordon Allport's (1954) intergroup contact hypothesis as an example of a prejudice-reducing tool—that if people from different racial groups were together and given a task that required cooperation, held equal status, and there was an acknowledged authority, this could reduce racial prejudice. All these criteria are met in the example of an integrated military, especially during wartime. Clearly, there is a common goal, an acknowledged authority, and equal status. Soldiers are also very clear that in order to win a battle and, ultimately, a war, cooperation with their fellow soldiers is required. A successful outcome can decrease racial prejudice. In fact, some research finds that the presence of a racially integrated military, even when not at war, has helped create an environment of high intercultural understanding, more interracial friendships, and improved attitudes toward racial outgroups (Leal 2003).

But what about intergroup contact more broadly; can it be a prejudice-reducing tool? Can integrating schools or neighborhoods or sports teams result in decreasing racial prejudice? If the individuals involved are placed in a competitive situation, racial hostility is likely to increase. However, positive contact between members of different racial groups can result in decreasing racial prejudice. It is more likely to successfully reduce prejudice if the participants take the perspective of the other, meaning they work at understanding the world from the perspective of people who are racially different from them (Sammut and Gaskell 2010).

Education is often promoted as a prejudice-reducing tool, with decades of research supporting this finding (Allport 1954; Heerwig and McCabe 2009; Hello, Scheepers, and Gijsberts 2002; Hello, Scheepers, and Steeger 2006; Meeusen, de Vroome, and Hooghe 2013; Wagner and Zick 1995). Specifically, educational attainment and racial prejudice are inversely related—the more education one has, the less racial prejudice they are likely to hold. Some have critiqued these findings, arguing that more highly educated individuals may simply be giving more socially desirable answers on surveys and that there is not actually a true relationship between educational attainment and racial prejudice. However, research has specifically tested this and found that the inverse relationship between education and racial prejudice is real (Wagner and Zick 1995). As scholar Charles Berg (2002:23) argues, "The antidote to stereotyping is knowledge"; learning about the Other and about the stereotyping process can reduce the effectiveness of stereotypes.

The prevalence of corporate and organizational diversity and cultural sensitivity training are examples of our belief that education can reduce prejudice. Police departments, the military, corporate America, and nonprofits across the country have implemented such training to improve relations with minority communities, create a more cooperative workforce, and increase their productivity. In general, though, education and short-term diversity training is never going to be enough to eradicate racism in our society. However, sociologist Victor Ray (2020:75) emphasizes the importance of studying prejudice, or psychological accounts of racism, because it remains "the cultural common sense" in our society. It can help us get beyond our socialization, see the stereotypes that we hold of others, and teach us to recognize that those are irrational. But since so much racism is structural rather than individual, addressing prejudice and stereotypes is not enough (see Chapter 4). Education is a necessary first step in eradicating racial prejudice, yet more work is needed to reach the goal of a racially just society.

Finally, much of the racial stereotype research that this chapter relies on emerges out of film and media studies, since "stereotyping in film can be seen as a graphic manifestation of the psychosocial process of stereotyping in society in general" (Berg 2002:4). Repetition reinforces stereotypes, so addressing the prevalence of stereotyping in the media is essential (Berg 2002). Thus, when considering how to reduce prejudice as part of the path toward a more racially just society, it is imperative that we look to diversifying media industries, specifically in leadership and decision-making positions.

Conclusion

This chapter explores the manifestation of racism as beliefs and attitudes, otherwise known as prejudice, and the extent to which such attitudes inform behaviors. Current research finds that racial prejudice manifests as aversive racism among otherwise liberals racialized as White and as racial resentment among political conservatives racialized as White. Racial prejudice has also long been connected to the perception that an out-group is a threat to one's group position. While decades of research finds declining racial prejudice, particularly in relation to increasing educational attainment, questions remain whether racial prejudice has truly declined or whether more educated people are giving more socially desirable answers. Finally, this chapter explores the predominant racial stereotypes for Asian Americans, African Americans, Latinxs, and Native Americans and a preponderance of ethnic stereotypes of Irish, Jewish, and Arab Americans. We end this chapter with a discussion of what the path to a more racially just society looks like, concluding that reducing or eradicating prejudice is merely a first step. A path to a more racially just society cannot be found with individual solutions like reducing prejudice; the objective is to eradicate structural racism, which we explore in the next chapter.

KEY TERMS AND CONCEPTS ————————

Aversive racism   44
Controlling images   52
Ethnocentrism   41
Intergroup contact hypothesis   43
Internalized racism   47
Model minority   47

Prejudice   41
Socialization   47
Stereotypes   46
White racial resentment   44
White space   48

CRITICAL THINKING QUESTIONS ————————

1. Try to recall when you first learned a racial stereotype, such as the idea that people racialized as Black are naturally gifted athletes, people racialized as Asian American are poor drivers, or people racialized as Latinx are lazy. Did you learn this through the telling of a joke, a knowing look between family members after a comment or story told about a

racial/ethnic group, or in a direct comment made by someone you love? Did you question the bias? Did it intuitively make sense to you? How did the context in which this was presented to you inform your interpretation of the stereotype? Have you questioned it since, or did it settle in and become real in your worldview?

2. Discuss some of the similarities between racial stereotypes attached to different racial minority groups. Why do you think this is? What do stereotypes of racial/ethnic minorities tell us about the dominant group, people racialized as White?

RECOMMENDED READINGS ────────────

Alport, Gordon. 1954. *The Nature of Prejudice*. Boston, MA: Addison-Wesley Press.

Berg, Charles Ramírez. 2002. *Latino Images in Film: Stereotypes, Subversion, and Resistance*. Austin, TX: University of Texas Press.

Bolge, Donald. 1994. *Toms, Coons, Mulattoes, Mammies, and Bucks: An Interpretive History of Blacks in American Films*, 3rd Edition. New York: Continuum.

Chou, Rosalind S. and Joe R. Feagin. 2008. *The Myth of the Model Minority: Asian Americans Facing Racism*. Boulder, CO: Paradigm Publishers.

Collins, Patricia Hill. 1990. *Black Feminist Thought: Knowledge, Consciousness, and the Politics of Empowerment*. New York: Routledge.

CHAPTER 4

Discrimination and Institutional Racism

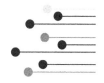

In this chapter, we continue our exploration of racism by looking at discrimination. While prejudice, discussed in the previous chapter, refers to attitudes or beliefs, discrimination refers to actions or behaviors. Generally, when we think of racism, examples of individual discrimination come to mind. **Individual discrimination** refers to overt, discriminatory actions taken against a member or members of a subordinate group because of their race. It is not hard to see Dylann Roof's, a man racialized as White, actions as an example of this type of racism. On June 17, 2015, he walked into the Emanuel African Methodist Episcopal Church in Charleston, South Carolina, and sat down with a group of Bible study participants racialized as Black. After approximately 30 minutes, he pulled out a handgun, shooting and killing nine of the people. It is also not hard to see the actions of a restaurant manager who refuses to hire Latinxs for front-of-the-house jobs, while eagerly hiring them to work in the kitchen, as racist and as an example of individual discrimination. These examples might lead us to assume three things about discrimination: that there is a clear perpetrator, there are clear and identifiable victims, and the actions are motivated by explicitly racist intentions. However, this is not always the case. In fact, the most prominent type of racism found in the United States today challenges what we think we know about racism because it refers to actions that go beyond the individual.

Institutional racism, sometimes referred to as *institutional discrimination*, refers to more covert types of discrimination, where everyday business practices and/or government policies result in disadvantage for people racialized as non-White and are advantageous to people racialized as White, regardless of intent. When sociologists use the term *institutional*, they are referring to "the interlocking sets of organizations that characterize larger domains . . . [such as] education, healthcare, or criminal justice, rather than a single school, hospital, or sheriff's department" (Hirschman 2020). Institutional racism can be found in an organization's hiring and firing practices, university admissions practices, government and organizational funding decisions, and the creation and enforcement of laws and social policies, and it is often understood as "just the way things are." This is the most prominent manifestation of racism in the United States today, as its operation melds well with the colorblind ideology (see Chapter 1).

Examples of institutional racism include the way public schools are primarily funded in the United States; the use of redlining by banks and insurance companies; the disproportionate presence of polluting industries near Black communities, known as **environmental racism**; and mass incarceration.

In each of these examples, there is no clear, individual perpetrator we can point to as "*the* racist"; instead, racial inequality is the outcome of the rules of the game and organizational processes, rather than the easily observable actions of an individual. Second, it is often hard to identify a victim of institutional racism; while there are many victims, it is not always clear they were victims of racism. For instance, public schools in the United States get about 45% of their funds from local personal property taxes. This results in vast inequality between schools along the lines of social class; schools in impoverished communities get fewer tax dollars, and schools in wealthier communities have considerably more tax dollars at their disposal. But since class and race overlap significantly in our society, poor schools are disproportionately composed of students racialized as non-White. Another problem with identifying a victim of racism in the example of school funding policies is that the disproportionate funding does not negatively impact all students equally. Some students racialized as Black from underfunded schools manage to get admitted to Ivy League institutions. Thus, one could argue that if they were not negatively affected by racism, then how can you argue their classmates were? Institutional racism is slippery like this. Finally, most institutional racism happens because of existing policies that are at least formally colorblind, so there appears to be no racist intent behind them. Certainly, one can look at the origins of racially disparate school funding formulas and find that racism was behind the initial decisions to underinvest in schools for children racialized as Black during the Jim Crow era, but you won't find that explicit rationale today to explain the school funding formula (Weinberg 1997). So the school funding formula is technically colorblind.

If institutional discrimination exists, then institutional privilege must also exist. The school funding formula that disadvantages schools with a student body disproportionately composed of students racialized as non-White shovels resources at schools with student populations predominantly racialized as White. **Institutional privilege** refers to the customs, norms, traditions, laws, and public policies that benefit people racialized as White (Williams 2003). In fact, critical race theorists argue that most White privilege takes the form of institutional privilege because it is maintained through policies and social structures (Williams 2003).

One can explore individual discrimination and institutional racism in any number of institutional settings—educational institutions, the media, the economic sphere, the political sphere, organized religion, and the criminal justice system. In this chapter, we are going to explore the ways racial discrimination manifests in two primary arenas: the economic sphere and the criminal justice system. (Unless otherwise noted, the statistics provided in this chapter do not capture the economic recession that accompanied the COVID-19 pandemic because the data did not yet exist.)

Racial Economic Inequality

Compared to other democratic, wealthy nations of the world, the United States is much more unequal. In addition to the dramatic levels of inequality in our society, this inequality is racialized. On key economic indicators, such as income, wealth, poverty, unemployment, and representation among corporate leaders, race matters tremendously. In a highly unequal society like the United States, there is going to be a certain percentage of people in poverty. When the data show that poverty rates are racialized, for instance, when people racialized as Native American face wildly disproportionate poverty rates compared to their percentage of the population, we conclude that this disparity cannot be a random occurrence.

The United States is one of the most unequal societies in the world, with vast disparities in wealth and poverty. Racial minorities are disproportionately impoverished.

Racial Inequality in Income and Wealth

Social scientists have documented a long-standing **racial wage gap**, which refers to differences in wages between workers racialized as White and workers racialized as African American, Latinx, and Native American, controlling for what is known as human capital—one's education, skills, and experience. Most of us operate on the assumption that our wages are set based upon the human capital we bring to an employer, but it turns out that being racialized as White or Asian American benefits workers economically while being racialized as African American, Latinx, or Native

American disadvantages workers. In 2018, median household income by race was as follows: White, non-Hispanic, $67,937; Black, $41,511; Asian American, $87,243; Hispanic, $51,404; and Native American, $40,315 ("Household Income: 2018" 2019) (see Figure 4.1).

Economists trying to explain the racial wage gap go beyond human capital and control for additional variables, including age, job type, and geography. Using these variables, in 1979, men racialized as Black earned 80 percent of what men racialized as White earned; in 2016, that differential had *widened*, with men racialized as Black earning only 70 percent of what men racialized as White earned. In 1979, women racialized as Black earned 95 percent of what women racialized as White earned, yet in 2016, they were only earning 82 percent of what women racialized as White earned. People racialized as Black and those racialized as White tend to work in different kinds of industries, which accounts for about 9 percent of the difference for men and 5 percent for women. Educational attainment accounts for about 5 percent of the difference for men and 5 percent for women. Ultimately, a significant chunk of the racial wage gap cannot be explained by standard variables and instead is classified by

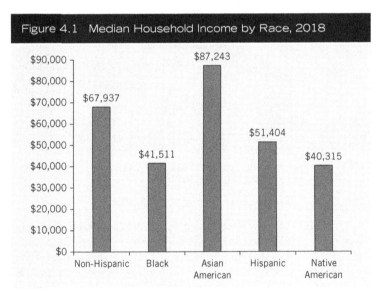

Figure 4.1   Median Household Income by Race, 2018

Source: Muhammad, Dedrick Asante, Rogelio Tec, and Kathy Ramirez. 2019. "Racial Wealth Snapshot: American Indians/Native Americans." NCRC National Community Reinvestment Coalition November 18. Retrieved June 17, 2020. (https://ncrc.org/racial-wealth-snapshot-american-indians-native-americans/).

economists as "unexplained," which could include racial discrimination (Daly, Hobijn, and Pedtke 2017).

Social scientists also compare racial groups in terms of wealth. Wealth refers to everything one owns, minus what they owe. So any money you have in your bank accounts or retirement account, stocks, and the equity you have in your home count as wealth. Wealth can be thought of as a cushion—wealth ultimately determines how long you can live at your current standard of living if you lost your income, a test many people faced during the COVID-19 pandemic. Wealth also accumulates over time and can be passed down from one generation to the next, creating advantages for future generations. Scholars have documented a long-standing **racial wealth gap**, which is the difference in wealth between median households by race. As of 2016, the median family racialized as White had $171,000 in wealth while the median family racialized as Black had $17,150, the median family racialized as Latinx had $20,700, and others (median households racialized as Asian American and Native American) had $64,800 (Ross 2020) (see Figure 4.2). Perhaps even more

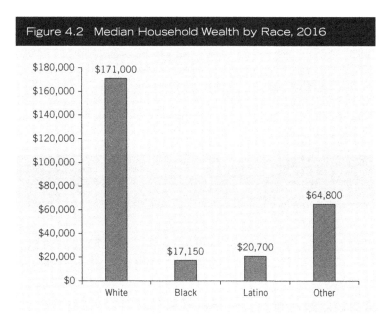

Figure 4.2   Median Household Wealth by Race, 2016

Source: Ross, Jenna. 2020. "The Racial Wealth Gap in America: Asset Types Held by Race." *Visual Capitalist* June 12. Retrieved June 17, 2020. (https://www.visualcapitalist.com/racial-wealth-gap/).

disturbingly, 19 percent of households racialized as Black have zero or negative net worth, compared to only 9 percent of White households with zero or negative net worth.

Most research finds that the bulk of the racial wealth gap cannot be explained by the racial wage gap (Altonji and Doraszelski 2005; Barsky et al. 2002; Blau and Graham 1990; Terrell 1971). The primary explanations have to do with differential rates of asset ownership—people racialized as White and Asian American are much more likely to own homes, have retirement accounts, and own stocks than people racialized as African American and Latinx (Ross 2020; see Table 4.1). Another variable is differential rates of intergenerational transfer, or inheritance, which is estimated to account for 5 to 20 percent of the wealth gap (Aliprantis and Carroll 2019; Gittleman and Wolff 2004; Menchik and Jianakoplos 1997).

Researchers have found that many of the individualistic explanations for the racial wealth gap simply do not hold up. For instance, some assume that the racial wealth gap merely reflects unequal educational attainment. However, "the median white adult who attended college has 7.2 times more wealth than the median black adult who attended college and 3.9 times more wealth than the median Latinx adult who attended college" (Oliver and Shapiro 2019). A second explanation offered is family structure; the fact that people racialized as African American have higher rates of single-mother families than people racialized as White is sometimes offered as an explanation for the racial wealth gap. However, the median single-parent household racialized as White has 2.2 times more wealth than a household racialized as Black with two parents and 1.9 times more than the median two-parent family racialized as Latinx (Oliver and Shapiro 2019). Some people consider wealth accumulation to be evidence of a thrifty personality, someone who

Table 4.1   Assets Held by Race, 2016

Assets	White	Black	Hispanic	Other
Primary residence	73	45	46	54
Vehicle	90	73	80	80
Retirement accounts	60	34	30	48
Family-owned business equity	15	7	6	13
Publicly traded stocks	61	31	28	47

Source: Ross, Jenna. 2020. "The Racial Wealth Gap in America: Asset Types Held by Race." Visual Capitalist June 12. Retrieved June 17, 2020. (https://www.visualcapitalist.com/racial-wealth-gap/).

avoids frivolous spending. Yet this explanation also falls short in explaining the racial wealth gap because households racialized as White spend more than households racialized as Black with similar incomes, so personal spending habits are not at the root of the racial wealth gap (Oliver and Shapiro 2019).

Sociologists focus on social policies that have facilitated White wealth accumulation and inhibited wealth accumulation among people racialized as Black, something referred as the **racialization of state policy** (Oliver and Shapiro 1995, 2019). The Homestead Acts, the GI Bill, and the Federal Housing Act are all examples of social policies that helped people racialized as White purchase homes, land, and businesses and denied these opportunities to people racialized as Black for generations (Oliver and Shapiro 2019). At the beginning of this chapter, we gave the example of bank redlining as an example of institutionalized racism. Redlining was a practice that realtors racialized as White insisted on being implemented in order for the Federal Housing Administration to approve government-backed mortgages, which was necessary to make home ownership attainable for the bulk of Americans (Rothstein 2017). **Redlining** is a practice where certain areas of the city, those overwhelmingly composed of populations of people racialized as Black, are defined as risky to creditors, resulting in banks being unwilling to lend to people living within these areas (Quadagno 1994). Redlining is an example of real estate industry practices that result in institutional discrimination. Limiting people racialized as Black from the opportunity of home ownership between the 1930s and the 1960s meant African Americans were denied two or more generations worth of wealth accumulation that people racialized as White had access to.

Poverty

In addition to the racial wage gap and the racial wealth gap, poverty is racialized in the United States. People racialized as African American, Latinx, and Native American are disproportionately impoverished, while people racialized as White are underrepresented among those in poverty. According to U.S. census data, in 2018, 10.1 percent of Americans racialized as White, non-Hispanic were impoverished, while 25.4 percent of people racialized as Native American, 20.8 percent of Blacks, 17.6 percent of Latinxs, and 10.1 percent of Asian Americans were impoverished ("The Population of Poverty" 2019) (see Figure 4.3).

As you can see from Figure 4.3, compared to their percentage of the population, people racialized as racial minorities face wildly disproportionate poverty rates while those racialized as White, non-Hispanics are underrepresented among those falling below the poverty line.

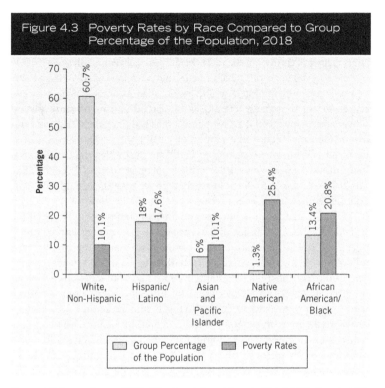

Figure 4.3 Poverty Rates by Race Compared to Group Percentage of the Population, 2018

Legend:
☐ Group Percentage of the Population   ■ Poverty Rates

Source: US Census Bureau 2017. "The Population of Poverty USA." 2018. Poverty USA. Retrieved Nov. 1, 2020 (https://www.povertyusa.org/facts).

Unemployment

Unemployment obviously changes in the face of larger fluctuations in the economy and external factors, such as the COVID-19 pandemic. But in every era, whether a strong economy or an economic recession, unemployment for people racialized as African American has remained stubbornly double the rates for those racialized as White, non-Hispanics. Due to the COVID-19 pandemic, unemployment rates in April of 2020 were 10 points higher than the previous month, at 14.7 percent, as discussed in Chapter 1. In 2018, overall unemployment was low, at 3.9 percent, yet racial disparities still existed. People racialized as African American had unemployment rates of 6.5 percent; Native Americans, 6.6 percent; Asian Americans, 3.0 percent; Hispanics, 4.7 percent; and Whites, 3.5 percent (see Figure 4.4; "Labor Force Characteristics" 2019). As noted previously, even in a strong economy, people racialized as African American have faced double the unemployment rates of people racialized as non-Hispanic White.

Figure 4.4 Unemployment by Race, 2018 and 2020, Pre-COVID and During COVID

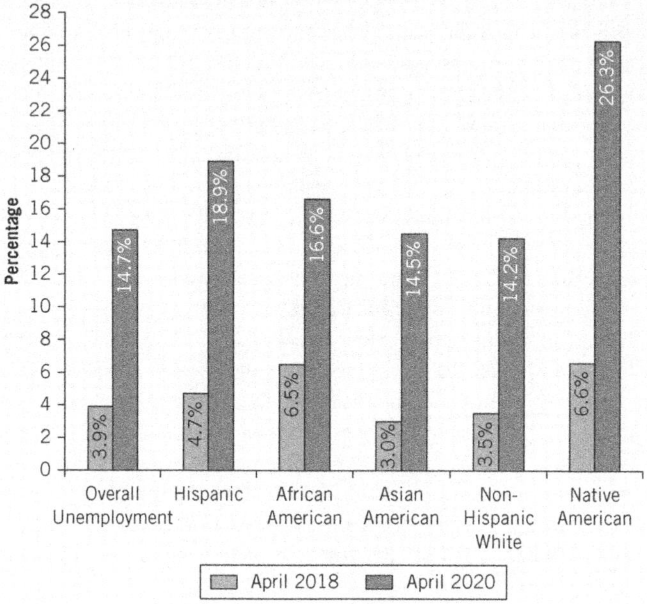

Data values by category:

Category	April 2018	April 2020
Overall Unemployment	3.9%	14.7%
Hispanic	4.7%	18.9%
African American	6.5%	16.6%
Asian American	3.0%	14.5%
Non-Hispanic White	3.5%	14.2%
Native American	6.6%	26.3%

Source: "Labor Force Characteristics by Race and Ethnicity, 2018." 2019. Bureau of Labor Statistics October. Retrieved July 22, 2020 (https://www.bls.gov/opub/reports/race-and-ethnicity/2018/home.htm#:~:text=The%20employment%E2%80%93population%20ratio%20was,%2C%205%2C%20and%205A.). Feir, Donna and Charles Golding. 2020. "Native Unemployment During COVID-19: Hit Hard in April, but Starting to Rebound?" Federal Reserve Bank of Minneapolis. Aug. 5. Retrieved Nov. 1, 2020 (https://www.min neapolisfed.org/article/2020/native-employment-during-covid-19-hit-hard-in-april-but-starting-to-rebound#:~:text=In%20April%202020%2C%20more%20than,Native%20unemployment%20rate%20for%20March).

Race, Corporate Leadership, and Media

As corporations respond to the global protests in support of Black Lives Matter and racial justice in 2020 by rebranding, removing offensive logos and slogans, and expressing support for racial justice through advertising and, in some cases, making financial contributions to racial justice organizations, the racial shortcomings of corporate America were also on full display. For instance, after 130 years in circulation, on June 17, 2020, Quaker Oats announced they were retiring the Aunt Jemima name, image, and packaging, due to its long-standing racist imagery. This image has long been offensive as it is "a caricature of black cooks . . . Based in blackface minstrel songs, the character, with her 19th century garb and head scarf, promoted a commodified version of antebellum imagery that valorized the enslavement of human beings" (Tipton-Martin 2020:ST7). Uncle Ben's rice, owned by Mars, Inc., followed suit the next day with a commitment to change the image on their packaging due to its racist connotations. A month prior to these announcements, Land O' Lakes butter announced they would remove the image of the Native American woman on their labels. Other corporations, including the makers of Mrs. Butterworth's syrup, have agreed to explore their brand image. It appears that, "in the past week, it seemed as if every major company has publicly condemned racism" (Gelles 2020).

So far, we have provided evidence that on most economic indicators, people racialized as racial minorities are disadvantaged while those racialized as White and, on some measures, those racialized as Asian American, are advantaged. We also have evidence of corporate America responding to the Black Lives Matter 2020 protests by changing racist imagery. But what about racial representation among corporate leadership? Are we anywhere near racial parity? The short answer is no. As of June of 2020, there were only four chief executives who are racialized as Black among the 500 largest companies in the country; there are no members racialized as Black on senior leadership teams in the technology world of Google, Facebook, Microsoft, or Amazon; similarly to the uber-White tech world, there are no

Justin Sullivan/Getty Images

In 2020, Quaker Oats announced they were retiring the Aunt Jemima image after 130 years in circulation. The image was long viewed as offensive because it was based on the enslaved mammy stereotype.

people racialized as African American on senior leadership teams in finance at Wells Fargo, JP Morgan Chase, or Bank of America; CVS has no people racialized as Black on its senior leadership team; ultimately, "at many of America's largest employers, black men and women are absent from meaningful leadership roles" (Gelles 2020).

Additionally, the media industry has long been critiqued for its lack of racial diversity (Flynn 2020). According to the News Leader Association, as of 2019, only 21.9 percent of salaried employees in newsrooms were people racialized as non-White (Flynn 2020). This influences not only what stories get covered but how they are framed. In the face of the 2020 racial justice uprisings, journalists racialized as non-White have started calling out their employers for racial insensitivity and racism in their news coverage. For instance, the *Philadelphia Inquirer* published a headline, "Buildings Matter, Too" that journalists racialized as racial minorities publicly reacted negatively to, resulting in the editors issuing an apology. At the *New York Times*, dozens of staffers protested an incendiary op-ed by Republican Senator Tom Cotton that called for the use of the military to calm the protests and that contained factual errors that would normally result in it not being published. The paper issued an apology, and a top editor resigned over the incident (Flynn 2020).

Racial Discrimination in the Economic Sphere

We have identified racial inequality in the economic sphere. Now we are going to explore the racism that contributes to these broader patterns of economic inequality; with decades of research on this topic, we will only be able to skim the surface. Prior to the passage of the Civil Rights Act of 1964, racial economic discrimination was blatant, engaged in openly in public, common, and unstigmatized (Gaddis 2019). One of the primary wins of the civil rights movement was the passage of the Civil Rights Act, which made racial discrimination, from the public sphere to employment, illegal. While a racist employer can no longer legally refuse to hire or promote a person racialized as non-White strictly on those grounds, discrimination continues despite its illegality for at least two reasons. One is that some people are more than willing to break the law. And second, as stated previously, most discrimination today is institutional discrimination, which is more covert and harder to prove due to the focus on intentionality in antidiscrimination law.

After the passage of this legislation, racial discrimination eventually became stigmatized, as people feared legal penalties, among other forms of backlash. This has had implications for researching racial discrimination as well, as survey and interview results were questioned. As with survey data on racial prejudice, scholars ask, are people being honest when they answer survey questions? Or do they simply hope to appear nonracist in their responses? Are interviews and surveys capable of capturing unconscious racism? (Gaddis 2019). Researchers turned to what are known as **audit studies**, a type of field experiment where you place two auditors, one racialized as White and the other racialized as non-White, in comparable settings, as job applicants or apartment seekers who are similar on paper and in appearance (other than race). You then observe how they are treated and document potential evidence of racial discrimination in employment, housing, and other arenas. Research consistently finds that auditors racialized as non-White are treated worse, meaning they are less likely to be called back for a job interview or they are denied the apartment they had applied for. This is assumed to be the result of discrimination because all variables other than race had been held constant (Bertrand and Mullainathan 2004). An overview of audit studies finds that hiring discrimination against people racialized as African American has remained steady since 1989 and discrimination against people racialized as Latinx has declined somewhat (Quillian, Pager, Hexel, and Midtbø 2017).

Sociologist Devah Pager's (2003) research employed an audit design to gauge the potential stigma of a criminal record on whether or not an employer called an applicant back, pairing male job seekers, one racialized as non-White and the other as White, applying for entry-level positions. The paired job seekers were identical on all measures, trading off the criminal record on different applications, which is known to be a major obstacle to employment. Her research found, astoundingly, that applicants racialized as White with a criminal record were called back more often than job seekers racialized as Black without a criminal record. Specifically, 34 percent of applicants racialized as White without a criminal record were called back after turning in their application, compared to only 17 percent of applicants racialized as White with a criminal record, showing that a criminal record acts as a substantial penalty to potential employment. However, the role of race was even more significant, as applicants racialized as Black without a criminal record were called back only 14 percent of the time, compared to the 17 percent callback rate for applicants racialized as White *with* a criminal record (Pager 2003).

Research by Marianne Bertrand and Sendhill Mullainathan (2004) sent fictionalized résumés to online job ads found in Chicago and Boston newspapers. The fake applicants sometimes had White-sounding names, like Emily or Greg, and at other times Black-sounding names, such as Lakisha or Jamal. This research found significant racial differences in callback rates;

specifically, employers were 50 percent more likely to call back applicants with White-sounding names; essentially, "a white name yields as many more call backs as an additional eight years of experience on a resume" (Bertrand and Mullainathan 2004:992). Additionally, they controlled for social class through addresses on the résumé, so that the applicants were not discriminated against along class lines. An address in a wealthy neighborhood helped the fictional applicants racialized as White a lot, but it did not help applicants racialized as Black more than those racialized as White. Also, the racial gap in callbacks holds across different occupations and industries (Bertrand and Mullainathan 2004).

Aside from audit studies, some scholars argue that racial discrimination in the job market is a result of **statistical discrimination**, which is when employers disregard individual applicants racialized as Black because of assumptions they make about urban workers racialized as Black in general (Wilson 1996). In other words, employers exhibit a preference for workers racialized as White based upon stereotypes they hold about racial minority workers (see Chapter 3). This means that individual applicants do not have a chance to prove themselves because stereotypes held by employers about their racial group's work ethic exclude them from consideration.

This was in effect in the rebuilding of New Orleans when 80 percent of the city was destroyed by flooding caused by levee breaches after Hurricane Katrina in 2005. Employers involved in rebuilding post-Katrina actively sought out workers racialized as Latinx. In 2000, only 3 percent of New Orleans's population was racialized as Latinx, yet nearly half the reconstruction workforce was Latinx. Employers went out of their way to acquire workers racialized as Latinx, despite the widespread unemployment among locals, because they believed people racialized as Latinx would be better at the work than local laborers racialized as Black (Skrentny 2014). When employers operate on these stereotypes, they are arguing that certain populations of people are better suited for low-skilled work because of abilities such as "diligence, the ability to maintain a positive and compliant attitude, the ability to work through pain or injury, and the ability to do boring and/or repetitive tasks without complaining" (Skrentny 2014:218). Thus, while the stereotypes held of workers racialized as Latinx advantaged them over those racialized as Black in the post-Katrina rebuilding employment opportunities, these stereotypes are clearly detrimental to both groups.

Finally, in order to understand economic inequality, we need to understand the ways White privilege plays out, in addition to the ways discrimination against people racialized as non-White operates. Sociologist Nancy DiTomaso (2013) argues that in order to understand racial economic inequality, it is essential to understand favoritism among people racialized as White.

This favoritism manifests in the form of **opportunity hoarding**, the various ways groups control access to resources, and the exchange of **social capital**, a set of informal values or norms that allow for cooperation between group members. Social capital can take the form of information, such as being told of a job opening that had not been publicly known to others or suggestions to a potential applicant as to what the employer may be looking for in a candidate, someone putting in a good word for you to the person doing the hiring, or personally knowing the person doing the hiring. In her research, DiTomaso (2013) found that respondents racialized as White explained that when they obtained good jobs, those with higher pay and benefits, they had to rely on their social networks—their friends, neighbors, and relatives who provided an inside track, an opportunity for them to get their foot in the door. The idea of social capital is connected to social solidarity, "who is likely to help whom" (DiTomaso 2013:69). People racialized as White justified this by arguing that once in the job, they had to prove themselves, without seeming to acknowledge that "perhaps there were blacks or other minorities who also might have wanted to get in the door and be able to prove themselves" (DiTomaso 2013:65). DiTomaso (2013) importantly points out that while exclusion is illegal because it is a form of discrimination, inclusion through opportunity hoarding or favoritism is perfectly legal.

Racism in the Criminal Justice System

Racial inequality in the criminal justice system is an outcome of both individual discrimination and institutional racism. As discussed in Chapter 3, stereotypes of people racialized as racial minorities often portray them as criminally inclined. Thus, one of the ways racism manifests throughout the criminal justice system is through the pervasiveness of such stereotypes that result in people racialized as non-White being more likely to be perceived as suspicious and criminally inclined and for them to have more encounters with police. An exploration of mass incarceration, the war on drugs, and police brutality, however, exemplifies how racism in the criminal justice system is not a result of a few bad apples, a few racists engaging in acts of individual discrimination, acting outside the norm. Instead, it shows institutional racism pervades the criminal justice system itself.

Mass Incarceration

Beginning in the mid-1970s, the United States began a destructive social experiment now known as **mass incarceration**, the comparatively and historically unique extreme rates of imprisonment, which

 on right margin: Justin Sullivan/Getty Images

The key characteristics of mass incarceration are the extremely high rates of imprisonment and the fact that men racialized as minorities make up the bulk of prisoners.

disproportionately ensnares people racialized as non-White. The United States is "the world's largest jailer, with 2.3 million people behind bars . . . with 5 percent of the world's population, we're home to 25 percent of its prison population" (Dreisinger 2016:8). Mass incarceration is an example of institutional racism, as the language of "law and order" and "get tough on crime" that set the stage for mass incarceration is colorblind, yet the enforcement of the law is decidedly racialized.

It is not only about who goes to prison that matters, but the ways a felony conviction is designed to permanently marginalize those bearing that stigma from mainstream society. Scholar Michelle Alexander (2010) argues persuasively that mass incarceration is the new Jim Crow—a system of social control designed to keep people racialized as Black and Brown subordinate and second-class citizens. Here are some of the parallels between the new Jim Crow and the old Jim Crow: In most states, people convicted of felonies lose their right to vote and serve on juries; they are marginalized in the economy as people with felony convictions are denied access to countless employment opportunities; they are denied access to public housing and welfare benefits they may otherwise qualify for; and they do not have access to student loans or grants that would give them access to higher education (Alexander 2010).

Research by sociologist Nicole Gonzalez Van Cleve (2016) finds that formally colorblind, presumably race-neutral court processes are instead dispensing **racialized punishment**, the ways racial meanings become embedded in the administration of justice, which, in practice, is about racial punishment before, during, and after the conviction of a defendant rather than about justice. She found that stereotypes of people racialized as Black and Brown as immoral, lazy, hypersexual, and undermotivated informed how court professionals interacted with them and the assumptions of guilt or innocence made about them. Throughout the courtroom interactions, people racialized as non-White were targets of abuse, while defendants racialized as White, especially those who were middle or upper class, were protected; "by providing special considerations, professionals created a segregated, privileged pipeline to channel wealthy white defendants into rehabilitation options or less-punitive alternatives like probation. This protected the white defendants' futures, which the professionals viewed as valuable" (Van Cleve 2016:66).

Immigrant Detention

Scholars have described a **crimmigration system**, referring to the merging of our criminal justice and immigration enforcement systems (Armenta 2017; Stumpf 2006). Immigrant detention is another racialized aspect of mass incarceration, as Latinxs are disproportionately targeted; since almost 80 percent of undocumented immigrants in the U.S. are Mexican or Central American, "restrictive immigration policies are the primary mechanism through which Latinxs are excluded and racialized in the United States" (Armenta 2017:83).

Mass incarceration is highly profitable due to the escalation of **prison privatization**, which is when states contract out correctional services or entire prisons to private businesses. Once this happens, the goal becomes profit, and the industry lobbies Congress to maintain or increase "get tough on crime" legislation. Like hotels, peak profits are made when prison beds are full, and the industry is always looking to expand into new markets to earn more profit. One of the markets private prisons have expanded into is immigrant detention. Corrections Corporation of America (CCA), now known as CoreCivic, is the largest private-prison operator in the U.S. They actively pushed Arizona legislators to pass SB 1070, Support Our Law Enforcement and Safe Neighborhoods Act, in 2010 which gave police the right to stop anyone that looked like an immigrant and check their papers (DuVernay 2016). This is part of the racialization of immigrants that was discussed in Chapter 2, as immigrants who are racialized as White are unlikely to come under suspicion of law enforcement. The passage of SB 1070 was quite lucrative for CCA as they held an exclusive contract with the state of Arizona to detain illegal immigrants, which was earning them $11 million per month as of 2015 (DuVernay 2016).

War on Drugs

The colorblind language of law and its racialized enforcement is most evident in the war on drugs, which began under President Nixon and was expanded tremendously by Presidents Reagan and Clinton. Sociologist Michael Tonry (1994:27) describes the effect of the war on drugs as having "unnecessarily blighted the lives of hundreds of thousands of young, disadvantaged Americans, especially black Americans." There are a number of ways the war on drugs is racialized. One is through racially disparate drug arrests, despite the fact that drug use does not vary by racial group. Specifically, 7.4 percent of people racialized as Black, 7.2 percent of people racialized as White, and 6.4 percent of people racialized as Latinx are drug users, which means that people racialized as non-Hispanic White compose, by far, the largest number of drug users in the country since Whites are such a large percentage of the U.S. population (61.6 percent) (Moore and Elkavich 2008). In 1976, people racialized as Black accounted for 22 percent of drug arrests while those racialized as White accounted for 77 percent. However, by 1993, people racialized as Black accounted for 40 percent of drug arrests, while those racialized as White accounted for 50 percent. During these years, people racialized as Black only made up around 12 percent of the U.S. population while those racialized as White made up 82 percent (Cooper 2015; Tonry 1994b). By 1996, people racialized as Black accounted for 62.6 percent of drug offenders in state prisons (Moore and Elkavich 2008).

Additionally, the type of drugs law enforcement focused on, specifically crack cocaine and heroin, were more likely found in low-income, minority communities, at least during the first decades of the drug war. In low income, urban communities, drug dealing is more likely to happen outdoors where it can be witnessed and the participants arrested, while suburban drug dealing is more likely to happen indoors; this privilege of privacy meant that more drug deals involving people racialized as White went undetected by law enforcement. Another reason is that as the number of arrests became a proxy for police officer productivity, police found arresting urban, poor people racialized as minorities was easier than arresting wealthier people racialized as White (Tonry 1994). Finally, racially disparate sentencing laws for powder cocaine, which was more commonly used by people racialized as White, and crack cocaine, which was more likely to be found in urban communities composed of people racialized as non-White, resulted in the war on drugs being much more punitive for people racialized as Black and Brown than for Whites. Specifically, federal laws punished crack offenses 100 times more severely than offenses involving powder cocaine. As Alexander (2010:109) explains, "A conviction for the sale of five hundred grams of powder cocaine triggers a five-year mandatory sentence, while only five grams of crack triggers the same sentences."

You might be thinking, well, what are we supposed to do, ignore drug dealing and drug use? If these people are breaking the law, what choice do we have? First, the origins of the war on drugs was not a response to a large-scale drug problem. Substance abuse rates had been declining throughout the 1970s. Second, the modern war on drugs announced by President Reagan in 1982 preceded the crack epidemic (Alexander 2010). It was not a response to a new, dangerous drug devastating urban communities. Additionally, addressing substance use and abuse through a criminal justice lens is only one possible approach to the problem. Another would be to take a public health approach. A **public health approach** to drugs is one that treats drug abuse as a health problem rather than a crime problem; such an approach would prioritize substance abuse treatment first, rather than spending societal resources incarcerating a drug user.

This approach might seem familiar to you if you are paying attention to the current opioid crisis. While the crack epidemic turned to punishment and incarceration of Americans racialized as Black as the solution, the opioid epidemic has inspired a more compassionate response, with an emphasis on drug rehabilitation for the victims who were overwhelmingly racialized as White (Frakt and Monkovic 2019). While the origins of the opioid crisis were in predominantly rural Appalachia and then shifted to the suburbs, both communities composed disproportionately of people racialized as White, it is a mistake to portray the crisis as affecting only people racialized as White. In 2017, people racialized as Black made up 12 percent of opioid-related overdose fatalities, people racialized as Hispanic accounted for 8 percent, while those racialized as non-Hispanic White accounted for the bulk of opioid-related deaths, at 78 percent of opioid-related deaths (Shihipar 2019).

Police Brutality

This book began with a discussion of the global protests during 2020 over police violence, triggered by the murder of George Floyd by a police officer. But of course, while George Floyd became a household name, he was not the only unarmed person killed by police in the first decades of the twenty-first century. According to data from Campaign Zero, almost 1,000 people are killed by police in the United States every year, and approximately 60 percent of them are unarmed ("The Problem" 2020). **Police brutality** is the use of excessive force by law enforcement, above what would be required to subdue a person. The Supreme Court has upheld much police violence. In *Graham v. Connor* (1989), the court argued that officers could use force "if doing so was 'objectively reasonable' from their point of view in the moment" (Bazelon 2020).

The origins of policing during the 1700s as slave patrols provide some insight into the racialized nature of the profession. Slave patrols (also known as paddyrollers) were the chief enforcers of the "legally sanctioned system of surveillance, intimidation, and brute force whose purpose was to control blacks" (Fountain 2018). The slave patrols were groups of armed men racialized as White who rode at night among the plantations seeking out runaway slaves, unsanctioned gatherings, weapons, contraband, and any signs of revolt (Fountain 2018).

Some scholars have identified links between the war on drugs and police brutality (Cooper 2015). As part of the war on drugs, millions of dollars were funneled into law enforcement; thousands of new police were hired, increasing the numbers of police nationwide by 26 percent; and police powers were increased primarily through the erosion of the Fourth Amendment and the Posse Comitatus Act (Cooper 2015). The erosion of the Fourth Amendment involved several key court decisions that expanded police powers. One included lowering the standard for allowing police to stop a civilian from "probable cause" to "reasonable suspicion," allowing police to engage in **pretextual traffic stops** that allow officers to stop someone for a minor offense and then to use that stop to search for drugs. Another made running from police a suspicious enough behavior that one could be stopped and searched simply for that behavior. Supreme Court Justice Thurgood Marshall called these decisions the "drug exception to the Constitution" (Cooper 2015; Powell and Hershenov 1990).

The Posse Comitatus Act was passed in 1878 and was intended to keep the military and police departments separate. Since the war on drugs, this act has been substantially eroded, allowing the military to provide police departments with equipment and to train police departments in using such equipment. President Reagan declared drugs to be a threat to national security, which opened the door to police and military cooperation even more. This has ultimately led to even small police departments having fully equipped SWAT teams, including grenade launchers, tanks, and semiautomatic weapons, increasing the likelihood of police officers viewing citizens as the enemy since they are, essentially, outfitted for war and wars require an enemy (Cooper 2015).

Scholars have argued that these erosions have contributed to more police brutality (Cooper 2015). These changes have resulted in a dramatic increase in stop and frisks, which result in psychological violence to citizens, from the unwarranted harassment to the verbal and physical abuse that can come with police–citizen interactions in a stop and frisk. While SWAT teams in the past were used for rare circumstances, such as a hostage negotiation, simply having the equipment has resulted in their increased use. They are now used to serve warrants for low-level drug possession charges and are involved in serving late-night, no-knock warrants, like the kind that killed Breonna Taylor in Louisville, Kentucky, in March 2020, while she was sleeping in her bed. SWAT teams are heavily armed and use a battering ram to enter the residence, resulting in much fear, chaos, and physical violence. According to the American Civil Liberties Union, it is usually households racialized as Black and Hispanic that are targeted by SWAT teams (American Civil Liberties Union 2014; Cooper 2015; Nunn 2002). Ultimately,

> by increasing the frequency of aggressive police/civilian
> interactions, stop and frisks increase the chances that violence
> will occur. This chance may be exacerbated if, consonant with
> the militarization of police departments, police officers have
> come to see civilians less as civilians they are charged to protect
> and more as the enemy . . . Moreover, when officers regularly
> treat civilians as enemies, civilians are less likely to comply
> with their orders, which may in turn further amplify violence.
> (Cooper 2015:1192)

Toward a More Racially Just Society

To begin with, there are systems in place to penalize racism in the economic sphere: Antidiscrimination laws exist, of course, such as affirmative action and Title VII of the Civil Rights Act of 1964, that specifically outlawed discrimination in employment. Research finds that such legislation has not altered the dominance of men racialized as White in the economic sphere (Stainback and Tomaskovic-Devey 2012). While antidiscrimination law is intended to protect against both individual discrimination and institutional discrimination, one of its limitations is its reliance on intentionality. Specifically, when someone claims they were discriminated against by an employer, they are making a claim of *disparate treatment*, which relies on proving the employer's discriminatory intent (Skrentny 2014). Since employers hire and fire numerous people, an accusation of racial (or gender) discrimination can be weakened when the employer has one person of color (or one woman) who they employ.

At the time of this writing, part of the protests against the most recent killing of a Black person by police, George Floyd, include calls to defund police as part of a path to a more racially just society. To **defund police** means "reallocating or redirecting funding away from police departments to other government agencies" (R. Ray, 2020). It is not synonymous with abolishing police, although there are people who are calling for that (Davis 2003). By redirecting funds away from police and to social service agencies, more appropriately trained personnel will respond to calls pertaining to mental illness, drug addiction, and homelessness (R. Ray 2020).

Conclusion
....

In this chapter, we explore discrimination, both individual and institutional, using two institutional arenas as examples: the economic sphere and the criminal justice system. We begin with evidence of racial inequality on all key economic indicators: income, wealth, poverty, and unemployment. Then, we explore racial inequality in corporate leadership, despite corporate America's symbolic embrace of racial justice in the wake of the 2020 protests sparked by the police killing of George Floyd in Minneapolis. We then introduce some of the most current research showing racial discrimination in the economic sphere, most specifically through audit studies. Our shift to discrimination in the criminal justice system looks at the ways mass incarceration, the war on drugs, and police brutality are all racialized, making racism in the criminal justice system institutionalized rather than the outcome of inappropriate behavior by a few "bad apples." We conclude the chapter with a discussion of defunding police as part of the path to a more racially just society.

KEY TERMS AND CONCEPTS ——————

Audit studies   70
Crimmigration system   74
Defund police   79

Environmental racism   59
Individual discrimination   59
Institutional privilege   60

CRITICAL THINKING QUESTIONS

1. Using the frame provided in this chapter for exploring racism within specific institutions, think about what racism and privilege look like in institutions *not* explored in this chapter: the educational or political spheres, media, or organized religion.

2. Tease out aspects of individual discrimination and institutional discrimination found in the criminal justice system and the economic sphere. Consider what the best way to address each is.

RECOMMENDED READINGS

Alexander, Michelle. 2010. *The New Jim Crow: Mass Incarceration in the Age of Colorblindness.* New York: The New Press.

DiTomaso, Nancy. 2013. *The American Non-dilemma: Racial Inequality Without Racism.* New York: Russel Sage Foundation.

Oliver, Melvin and Thomas Shapiro. 1995. *Black Wealth/White Wealth: A New Perspective on Racial Inequality.* New York: Routledge.

Van Cleve, Nicole Gonzalez. 2016. *Crook County: Racism and Injustice in America's Largest Criminal Court.* Stanford, CA: Stanford Law Books.

Interracial Intimacies

In this chapter, we explore interracial intimacies, a topic that covers interracial relationships, multiracial families, and biracial/multiracial identities. Essentially, we look at how the most intimate aspects of our lives are influenced—and sometimes governed—by cultural understandings of race and racism. The status and extent of interracial relationships in a society and the potential obstacles faced by individuals in interracial relationships, multiracial families, and/or biracial/multiracial people can be gauges for evaluating the level of racism in that society. The extent of assimilation, described in Chapter 2, is understood as a proxy for societal race relations (Yancey and Lewis 2009). Milton Gordon (1964) identified seven stages of assimilation, the third of which he referred to as **marital assimilation**, also known as **amalgamation**, the point where widespread intermarriage is accepted, normal, and uncontroversial. Until Americans confront racial bias in the most intimate arenas of our lives, there is no hope of us becoming a racially just society. As Rachel Moran (2001:196) optimistically argues, through interracial intimacy, "we can undo race before it undoes us."

Bettmann/Getty Images

Mildred and Richard Loving are the interracial couple behind the 1967 Supreme Court decision *Loving v. Virginia* that legalized interracial relationships nationwide.

It was not that long ago that an interracially married couple, Richard and Mildred Loving, found police pounding on their door in the middle of the night to arrest them for violating Virginia's antimiscegenation law. Richard, a man racialized as White, and Mildred, a woman racialized as Black with both Native American and African American ancestry, had married in Washington, D.C., where it was legal, but they returned to their home in a small, rural community in Virginia to live their lives. They pled guilty, were convicted, and were sentenced to one year in prison, a sentence which was suspended for 25 years in exchange for them leaving the state of Virginia. This case eventually became the Supreme Court case *Loving v. Virginia* (1967) that overturned the remaining 16 state **antimiscegenation laws,** laws that made interracial relationships and interracial sex illegal. Such laws, however, were even more restrictive than that; they went so far as to make it illegal for a person racialized as Black and a person racialized as White to share a room after dark (Kennedy 2003).

Between 1660 and 1967, 41 states and territories had implemented antimiscegenation laws; all prohibited interracial sex and marriage between people racialized as Black and those racialized as White, but some also stipulated that people racialized as Chinese, Japanese, Native American, and Mexican, among others, were prohibited from marrying people racialized as White. The impetus for passing antimiscegenation laws seems to be when the population of people racialized as Black in the state or territory reached 5 percent; at that point, they were deemed enough of a threat that antimiscegenation laws were considered by people racialized as White to be necessary (Kennedy 2003).

All societies engage in **social control**—efforts to limit deviance and encourage conformity to the laws and norms. Antimiscegenation laws are an example of **formal social control**, when social control efforts are codified, written into rules or laws that make it easier to punish those who violate the rules. Sanctions for violating laws and rules are also codified—whether violation of a law can result in incarceration, for instance, or whether violation of a rule at work can result in termination. Efforts to limit deviance can also be informal; **informal social control** refers to the actions or interactions designed to get people to conform to the unwritten expectations about behavior, known as norms. Sanctions for violating norms are very different from those for violating laws and codified rules; they are actions taken to let people know they are violating expectations; they act much like peer pressure. In the past, lynching was an example of a form of punishment directed at men racialized as Black who were accused of having sex with a woman racialized as White. Today, when an interracial couple is glared at in public, for instance, or when a family rejects a member who is dating someone of a different race, or when a person is verbally harassed at work for being married to someone of a different race, all of these are examples of informal social control, the kinds of sanctions that are imposed on people who violate norms.

They are informal, so violating the rules won't get you sent to prison, yet they are quite powerful in their effect.

Why is there so much hostility toward interracial relationships? Why go to such lengths to prohibit them? The reasons most often provided include religious arguments—that God created separate races, and thus, they should remain that way. Another widely expressed concern, historically and currently, is embedded in the question, "What about the children?" This question implies that children racialized as biracial/multiracial, an expected outcome of inter- racial relationships, will face such hostility and harassment that it is not fair to bring them into the world. Hostility from people racialized as White toward interracial relationships has been related to the idea that the partner racialized as White's superior status is diluted by their relationship with someone of a subordinate racial status. There is also often resistance from minority commu- nities to one of their own marrying a person racialized as White. Sometimes, this is viewed as them losing touch with their culture and their identity; other times, it has to do with the history of racial oppression. Finally, the most com- mon argument for implementing antimiscegenation laws was that they were designed to protect the "purity" of the group racialized as White. The entire racial hierarchy rests on the idea that there are distinct races and that they exist on a hierarchy; thus, interracial relationships, multiracial families, and biracial/ multiracial people blur those distinctions, diminishing the power of the racial hierarchy, which disadvantages those who benefit the most from that hierarchy: those racialized as White.

Interracial Relationships
....

Most research on interracial relationships focuses on those racialized as Black–White relationships, despite the fact that Black–White marriages are among the most uncommon and the statistical data on the extent of interracial marriages includes all interracial relationships, including those racialized as Asian American–White, White–Hispanic, Hispanic–Black, White–Native American, and so forth (see Figure 5.1). One reason offered for focusing on interracial marriages racialized as Black–White in research is that Blacks are the only group who have been held to the one-drop rule, where any Black ancestry dictated that someone legally and socially be recognized as Black (see Chapter 1). A second reason is that people racialized as White are the only group to which an idea of racial purity is applied, however illogically. Antimiscegenation laws were not written to prohibit people racialized as Black from marrying people racialized as Latinx or Native American or any other person of color; "intermarriage among persons of color does not challenge the existing hierarchy of races in which 'pure' white is the pinnacle" (Korgen 1998:2). Also, while antimiscegenation laws applied to many groups, only people racialized as Blacks were included in such legislation across the board. So antimiscegenation laws have disproportionately prohibited relationships racialized as Black–White. As sociologist Amy Steinbugler (2012:xiii) explains, "This color line has historically been the most rigorously surveilled and restricted." Finally, relationships racialized as Black–White tell us the most about the extent of racism in our society (Dalmage 2000). Ultimately, "it is the mixing of white and nonwhite blood that makes (and has made) many Americans feel uncomfortable" (Korgen 1998:1–2).

In the United States, most marriages are **endogamous**, meaning most people marry someone from their own group, whether religious, racial, or social class. Despite this fact, interracial marriage has steadily increased

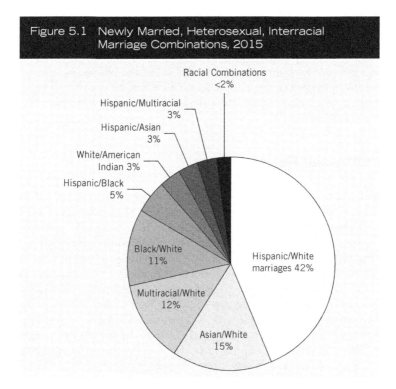

Figure 5.1 Newly Married, Heterosexual, Interracial Marriage Combinations, 2015

Source: "About One in Five Couples . . ." https://www.pewsocialtrends.org/2017/05/18/1-trends-and-patterns-in-intermarriage/

since 1967, when the Supreme Court overturned the final legal prohibitions on such marriages in *Loving v. Virginia*. In 1967, 3 percent of all marriages were interracial, 4.5 percent were interracial in 1990, 6.8 percent were in 2000, 8.4 percent were in 2010, and 10 percent were interracial in 2015; importantly, 17 percent of newly married couples in 2015 were in an interracial relationship (Bialik 2017) (see Figure 5.2). Keep in mind that after 1967, all formal social control prohibiting interracial marriages had been overturned, so informal social control efforts were and are to be understood as still very effective at keeping endogamy the norm.

The prior data only refer to interracial marriage, not interracial dating. Research finds that dating exclusively within one's racial group is strong among all racial groups (Blackwell and Lichter 2004; Joyner and Kao 2005; Robnett and Feliciano 2011). People engage in exclusionary dating practices all the time. One example is who we include in our dating pool, which simply refers to "the group of people a person is disposed to date" (Mitchell and Wells 2018:947). For most people, their dating pool is limited along the lines of sex/gender; some people will only date members of the opposite sex, other people prefer to date people who are their same sex, and for still other people, sex/gender are not exclusionary factors at all. Many people also maintain racial exclusion practices when considering their dating pool, yet this is established using the language of "romantic preferences" or "romantic attraction" rather than stating, "I don't date Black people," which would be unacceptably racist. They claim, "I am just not attracted to Black

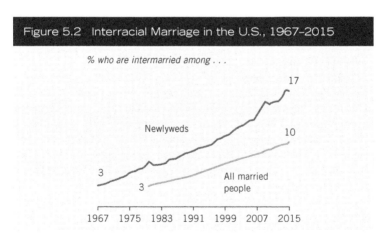

Figure 5.2 Interracial Marriage in the U.S., 1967–2015

% who are intermarried among . . .

17

Newlyweds

10

3

3

All married people

1967 1975 1983 1991 1999 2007 2015

Source: Pew Research Center. "Interracial Marriage in the US, 1967–2015," https://www.pewresearch.org/fact-tank/2017/06/12/key-facts-about-race-and-marriage-50-years-after-loving-v-virginia/

people." When understood within its larger social and historical context, particularly the long history of antimiscegenation laws and the valorization of Whiteness and Eurocentric features as the epitome of beauty, "With respect to racialized romantic dating preferences, perhaps not all racialized romantic discrimination against people of color has a disrespectful social meaning, but a lot of it does" (Mitchell and Wells 2018:954).

In a study of Internet dating ads, Robnett and Feliciano (2011) find that race and gender play significant roles in dating preferences. For instance, people racialized as White are far more likely to exclusively date other people racialized as White, while those racialized as Asian American, Black, and Latinx are more open to dating people racialized as White than Whites are to dating them. People racialized as Asian American and Latinx are more likely to exclude people racialized as Black, while being open to people racialized as White, Asian American, and Latinx. People racialized as Hispanic or Latinx are more inclusive of dating people racialized as Black than are people racialized as White or Asian American (Robnett and Feliciano 2011).

When gender is factored into the equation, racial exclusion practices become quite complicated. Men racialized as White, for instance, exclude women racialized as Black 97 percent of the time, exclude women racialized as Asian American 53 percent of the time, and are the most open to dating women racialized as Hispanic/Latinx yet still exclude them from their dating preferences 48 percent of the time. Women racialized as Black exclude men racialized as White from their dating preferences 75 percent of the time, and 33 percent of women racialized as Hispanic exclude men racialized as White, while only 11 percent of women racialized as Asian American exclude men racialized as White as potential dating partners (Robnett and Feliciano 2011).

Gender gaps in interracial marriage are also prevalent; for instance, men racialized as Black are twice as likely as women racialized as Black to be interracially married. The gender gap runs in the opposite direction for those racialized as Asian American, with approximately 36 percent of women racialized as Asian American marrying someone of a different race, compared to 21 percent of men racialized as Asian American. There is no gender gap in interracial marriage for people racialized as White or Latinx (Livingston and Brown 2017).

A number of studies have found that men racialized as Asian and women racialized as Black rank as the least desirable among heterosexual online daters (Buggs 2017; Feliciano, Robnett, and Komaie 2009; Lin and Lundquist 2013; Lundquist and Lin 2015; Robnett and Feliciano 2011; Rudder 2014; Tsunokai, McGrath, and Kavanagh 2014). These findings suggest the presence of **sexual racism**, when our preferences for possible romantic partners reflect and reinforce the existing racial hierarchies and racial stereotypes (Bedi 2014). In effect, "racialized social standards of beauty, sex appeal, and who makes good 'dating material' disrespect people of color" (Mitchell and Wells 2018:958).

Navigating the Racial Divide

Most of the sociological research on interracial relationships is focused on how partners navigate the racial divide, since neighborhoods, schools, friendship circles, and churches are still overwhelmingly racially segregated. As discussed previously, interracial relationships draw considerable attempts at regulation, from formal social control efforts in the past to informal social control efforts that remain today. Efforts at informal social control are really about **boundary maintenance**—efforts to maintain distinct racial groups (Childs 2009).

Boundary maintenance is maintained through **border patrolling**—informal sanctions that send the message that people should "stick with their own kind," that interracially dating or forming a multiracial family are against the rules and inappropriate (Dalmage 2000). While people racialized as White have been the most hostile to interracial relationships, presumably because it destabilizes the racial hierarchy and, thus, is a threat to White privilege, people racialized as Black also engage in border patrolling, albeit for different reasons. Border patrolling for people racialized as White is about maintaining White superiority, which the transgressor, who is viewed as "polluted," threatens through dating interracially or through forming an interracial family. People racialized as Black engage in border patrolling as a way to signal their race loyalty and another's lack of such loyalty; they send the message to people racialized as Black who date or marry interracially that they have lost their culture and identity through such actions (Dalmage 2000). In both cases, this border patrolling makes life uncomfortable and difficult for people in relationships racialized as interracial and for multiracial families; indeed, that is the goal of border patrolling.

Sociologist Ruth Frankenberg studied women racialized as White who were in interracial relationships, both same-sex and heterosexual relationships. She found that being in such an intimate relationship with a person of color gave them considerable insight into the racism and discrimination people racialized as non-White face and specifically challenged their embrace of colorblindness (see Chapter 1). She identified a phenomenon referred to as **rebound racism**, which captures the partner racialized as

White's pain associated with seeing racism and hate directed at their loved one, whether it's their partner who is racialized as non-White or their biracial/multiracial child. Like a rebound in basketball, the sting is less intense for the partner racialized as White than it is for the person of color who it is directed at. Nevertheless, seeing racism directed at someone you love dearly is deeply painful.

Sociologist Amy Steinbugler (2012:xiii) focuses on what she calls **racework**—"the routine actions and strategies through which individuals maintain close relationships across lines of racial stratification" in her study of lesbian, gay, and heterosexual couples racialized as Black–White. The term *racework* is meant to capture the extra labor involved in maintaining an interracial relationship. She identifies four types of racework: boundary work, visibility management, emotional labor, and navigating racial homogeneity. In this chapter, we elaborate on one of these types of racework, navigating racial homogeneity, which refers to the energy partners expend deciding what types of environments each partner is going to feel comfortable in, from churches to neighborhoods to holiday parties. Ultimately, "Black partners in majority-White spaces and White partners in majority-Black spaces both experience racial fatigue. They contend with the stress of always feeling conspicuous and of having to attend to the presence of racial undercurrents in everyday social interactions" (Steinbugler 2012:19). This racial fatigue, however, is not equivalent because of the existence of White privilege, which provides some comfort, even in a non-White context. Steinbugler's work also points out that queer spaces have historically been and remain racially segregated as well, providing unique challenges to same-sex couples racialized as interracial. Lesbians racialized as Black, for instance, might engage in border patrolling to create spaces that are safe from homophobia and racism; creating such a space where they are comfortable sometimes requires an understandable exclusivity, which limits options for lesbian couples racialized as Black–White to participate (Steinbugler 2012).

Interracial Relationships in Popular Culture

Portrayals of interracial relationships have hinged upon a long history of sexual racism targeting people racialized as non-White. For instance, European constructions of indigenous people as inferior involved accusations of sexual deviancy as part of their racialization. Women racialized as Indigenous were described as lustful, which allowed for interracial relationships and nonconsensual sex, or rape, between male European colonizers racialized as White and Indigenous females racialized as non-White to be understood as the women's fault. European colonizers racialized as White who first encountered Africans sexualized them as well, describing them as lustful, deviant, and as having extremely large genitalia (Childs 2009; McClintock 1995; Jordan 1968). Such sexual racism extended into slavery and the Jim Crow era, with people racialized as Black portrayed as animalistic, sexual savages, promiscuous, and immoral (Childs 2009). Again, the sexual racism functioned to justify the sexual exploitation of women racialized as Black and the violence directed at men racialized as Black.

Sociologist Erica Chito Childs (2009:2) studied interracial relationships in popular culture, including television, film, sports, and music, and in coverage of high-profile news events. She argues that images of interracial sex "both shape and are shaped by contemporary attitudes about race and sex in the United States today." Childs argues that interracial relationships primarily suffer from invisibility in popular culture, but when they are present, there are three main frames through which they are presented. The first is a deviant frame; they are portrayed as problematic relationships that range from temporary hookups to dangerous encounters, usually involving an unstable woman racialized as White. In the second frame, representations of interracial relationships tend to privilege, protect, and empower Whiteness. This involves emphasizing the goodness of people racialized as White or White society; men racialized as White, for instance, are seen as saving women racialized as Black or Brown from their communities. The third frame Childs (2009) identifies is that racism is both denied and perpetuated in popular culture portrayals of interracial relationships. The very presence of interracial relationships in the media is presented as evidence that we are postracial; however, the portrayals are still racist. For instance, communities of color are portrayed as being resistant to interracial relationships, while communities racialized as White are portrayed as welcoming. (There can be individuals racialized as White who oppose the union and are portrayed as racists, but the White community is viewed as supportive [Childs 2009].)

Despite the critiques of popular culture portrayals of interracial relationships discussed before, some research uses the **extended contact hypothesis** to argue that mass-media portrayals of Black–White interracial relationships may be associated with more positive attitudes toward interracial relationships (Lienemann and Stopp 2013). The extended contact hypothesis builds on Allport's (1954) intergroup contact hypothesis, discussed in Chapter 3; it is the idea that if exposure to an out-group increases over time, it can lead to greater empathy for the out-group, as well as increased trust for them, among other benefits (Lienemann and Stopp 2013; Paolini, Hewstone, and Cairns 2007; Pettigrew and Tropp 2008; Tam et al. 2008).

Multiracial Families

Studying multiracial families' experiences can help us understand our society because "multiracial family members spend a great deal of time talking, thinking, and theorizing about race. They must. As visible indicators that the color line has been breached, they become lightning rods for racial thoughts, actions, and discussions" (Dalmage 2000:33). Multiracial families face border patrolling, from both people racialized as White and racial minorities; face issues navigating our racially divided world; and are less protected by antidiscrimination laws.

Despite the presence of antimiscegenation laws, there have always been people who fell in love with people who they were legally prohibited from being with, so multiracial families have always existed, even during slavery. While many feminist scholars, including Angela Davis (1981), have argued that consensual relationships between slaves and free White people were not possible because the enslaved person could hardly refuse, Harvard law professor Randall Kennedy (2003) disagrees. Kennedy (2003:45) argues that "we can still be sensitive to the plight of enslaved women, however, and still acknowledge that consensual sex, prompted by erotic attraction, and other mysteries of the human condition, has occurred between subordinates and superiors in even the most barren and brutal settings." Kennedy documents numerous examples of interracial relationships during slavery and Jim Crow—the years such relationships were legally prohibited—that appear to be based upon love and companionship, despite the extreme status inequities between the partners. One example was of a prosperous Virginia plantation owner and Revolutionary War hero, Ralph Quarles, who entered into a relationship with Lucy Langston, his slave who he acquired as payment for a debt. Per the dictates of his will, upon death, they were buried together in 1834. Quarles and Langston had four children together that he financially supported, and he emancipated all five members of his multiracial family upon his death (Kennedy 2003).

Multiracial families have faced considerable harassment, from lynching in the past to social exclusion and microaggressions today (Onwuachi-Willig 2013; Romano 2003; Spickard 1989; Yancey and Lewis 2009). As sociologists argue, "while sexual activity amongst unmarried interracial individuals was not typically seen as desirable, it was more accepted than interracial marriage, which institutionalized a union between two people in civil or religious terms and made it a formal part of society" and, of course, is the foundation for the emergence of multiracial families (Yancey and Lewis 2009:3).

One of the primary privileges monoracial families face is in housing, housing choice, and the application of antidiscrimination law (Dalmage 2000; Onwuachi-Willig 2013). Most residential neighborhoods, for instance, are not racially integrated; in fact, the housing market has been described as hypersegregated (Massey and Denton 1993; Rothstein 2017). The fact that suburbs are overwhelmingly populated by people racialized as White and urban areas are overwhelmingly populated by people racialized as Black and Brown has not been accidental but, rather, is linked to a long history of institutionalized racism in the housing market (Rothstein 2017). In fact, "in the housing market, whiteness is constructed as inherently valuable" (Dalmage 2006:304). While this has resulted in advantages for people racialized as White in terms of home ownership and wealth accumulation (see Chapter 4) and families racialized as Black and Brown are disadvantaged, it has also resulted in unique and often overlooked challenges for multiracial families. Like every family, multiracial families hope for a community where they feel a sense of belonging, so a racially integrated community is ideal; however, there are not a lot of truly racially integrated communities in the United States. The integrated, multiracial communities that do exist in the U.S. are generally professional, middle-class to upper-middle-class communities that exclude many families based upon social class. So, a Black–White multiracial family is going to find themselves choosing between a community racialized as White or a community racialized as Black, both with their disadvantages in terms of comfort level for all members of the household.

Multiracial families face segregation imposed by institutions controlled by people racialized as White, and in neighborhoods racialized as Black, they face border patrolling from all sides (Dalmage 2000). People of all races engage in border patrolling directed at people in interracial relationships and those in multiracial families; as mentioned previously, border patrollers believe that people should stick to their own kind. Research finds that, especially during the 1960s and '70s era of Black power, multiracial families faced resistance when they sought to live in communities racialized as Black; "Multiracial families that formed after the late 1970s tell a story of guarded acceptance, albeit on easier terms" (Dalmage 2000:82).

The existence of antimiscegenation laws means that not only did the law prohibit interracial relationships but also that it defined multiracial families in ways that are discriminatory; in other words, in the eyes of the law, the normative family is monoracial (Onwuachi-Willig 2013). The case *Rhinelander v. Rhinelander* (1924) dramatically exposes this. In this case, Alice was a racially ambiguous working-class woman who met and fell in love with a wealthy man racialized as White, Leonard Rhinelander. After dating for three years, they married in 1924. After two months, Leonard filed for an annulment, claiming Alice had committed race fraud—that she had misled him by telling him she was White and not "colored." According to the story, Leonard's father forced the lawsuit because he did not approve of the marriage. Leonard, who by all accounts dearly loved Alice, encouraged her to fight to prove she was White. Case law is full of cases where people went to court to prove they were White; in fact, decisions in such lawsuits are part of the racialization process of racially ambiguous people in the United States. Alice refused to fight to prove her Whiteness and instead argued that Leonard knew exactly who and what she was when they married. In this case, the court found in favor of Alice, that there was no way Leonard could not have known she was not White. This decision ended their marriage by defining them as a multiracial family, which, at the time, was illegal in most states and against the norm throughout the country. This story exemplifies the marginality of multiracial families historically, a marginality that partially remains in the law in the current era (Onwuachi-Willig 2013).

Something less often recognized is that members of multiracial families often face workplace discrimination, from loss of jobs to social mistreatment and harassment on the job (Dalmage 2000; Onwuachi-Willig 2013). Employees racialized as White with multiracial families face sexual innuendos from coworkers and racist taunts about their biracial/multiracial children. Many people racialized as White have filed lawsuits against their employers for such discrimination, yet the courts have often not found the claim of their discrimination based upon their interraciality valid. In the cases in which the plaintiffs have won based upon the "discrimination by association" they experienced, the law has failed to recognize the effect of such discrimination on the collective, or the couple, which would recognize interraciality in antidiscrimination law (Onwuachi-Willig 2013). For instance, many high-powered jobs contain unwritten rules that require considerable public support from the employee's spouse and family. In a world where monoraciality is the norm, being in a multiracial family can inhibit a person's career trajectory in such cases. Because of the way antidiscrimination law is written, what judges "do not recognize are the harms that stem from prejudice against workers in interracial couples where unwritten job requirements and functions extend beyond the official job description and into the family" (Onwuachi-Willig 2013).

Transracial Adoption

In addition to an interracial couple and their children forming what we refer to as multiracial families, such families are also formed through transracial adoption. Historically, transracial adoption was illegal, one of the ways that monoracial families were legally sanctioned and idealized as the norm. In fact, early adoption policy sought to match adoptive children with parents of similar physical, social, religious, and intellectual backgrounds. The logic behind this was that such similarities would increase the chance of parent–child bonding and identification (Yancey and Lewis 2009). In the court case *Green v. The City of New Orleans*, a child was born to a mother racialized as White and given up for adoption, and a family racialized as African American, the Greens, hoped to adopt. Since the child had a birth mother who was racialized as White, the state denied the adoption on the grounds that the baby might be White, and transracial adoptions and multiracial families were illegal in Louisiana in 1952, when this case was heard. In this case, "the state believed, in other words, that it was better for a child to be reared in an institution, no matter how bad, than to be adopted into a family of a different race, no matter how good" (Kennedy 2003:12). In the 1950s, the one-drop rule dictated adoptions so that even biracial children were placed in households racialized as Black (Yancey and Lewis 2009).

Even today, without prohibitions on transracial adoption, many people simply prefer to adopt children of their own race. Since there is a racial imbalance in the adoption market, people racialized as White dominate the adopting parents market, and children racialized as Black dominate the children market; "this makes White children more easily placed than children of color since there are more White families per White child than families of color per child of color waiting to adopt" (Yancey and Lewis 2009:131). Adoption agencies have addressed this by making the adoption of children of color easier, providing incentives for families racialized as White to transracially adopt. As of 2010, 28 percent of adopted children in the U.S. were placed with a parent of a different race; that increases to 4 in 10 when Hispanic children and families are included (Cashin 2017).

There has been considerable resistance to transracial adoption, from both Native American tribes and the National Association of Black Social Workers. They dispute the argument made by adoption agencies that there are not enough minority parents willing to adopt. Instead, they argue that Eurocentric criteria for judging family fitness exclude willing and able families of color from adopting. They also argue that families racialized as White who adopt children racialized as non-White may mean well, but they are unable to meet the needs of these children (Yancey and Lewis 2009). Ultimately, there is no research evidence to support the argument that children racialized as Black adopted into families racialized as White are harmed by living in a multiracial family.

Of course, simply being racialized as White does not mean someone is unable to understand the racial needs of a child racialized as non-White. It does mean one has to work toward understanding the role of race and racism in that child's life and not approach it through the typical colorblind lens that dominates racial socialization of people racialized as White. As scholar Sheryll Cashin (2017:158) explains, "When a new biracial or multiracial family is created through adoption, whether the parent is ready for it or not, the adult should have racial dexterity or be willing to acquire it.

Amelie Kindler

In the last few decades, there has been an increase in interracial relationships, multiracial families, and people identifying as biracial/multiracial. Multiracial families, like the one pictured here, face unique dilemmas navigating a racially segregated world.

Social science research suggests that color blindness is a recipe for damage. Eventually, parenting and loving a son or daughter of a different race forces the adult to see race and racism."

Biracial/Multiracial Identities

As noted previously, interracial relationships have been increasing, particularly among millennials, and thus, we are seeing a corresponding rise in multiracial families and their children racialized as biracial/multiracial. As of 2015, approximately 6.9 percent of adults in the United States identify as biracial/multiracial, up from 2.9 percent in 2010; multiracial Americans are growing 3 times as fast as the overall population (Goo 2015).

Biracial/multiracial people have always existed, of course, due to interracial relationships that occurred despite prohibitions and due to the rape of slave women by White slave owners. However, the presence of the one-drop rule and the rule of hypodescent (see Chapter 1), which were legally enforced for generations, meant that people born of such unions had to identify as Black or as the subordinate racial status; "prior to the 1960s, biracial identity was equivalent to black identity" (Rockquemore and Brunsma 2002:21). In other words, biracial/multiracial *people* have always existed, but biracial/multiracial *identities* have not. This was true throughout the United States except for two locations where the one-drop rule was rejected: Louisiana and South Carolina, where both recognized an in-between racial status. In Louisiana, they were known as Creoles of Color and in South Carolina they were known as mulattos; in both cases, they had higher status than people racialized as Black while they had lower status and fewer privileges than people racialized as White (Davis 1991). Historically, people racialized as mulattos, or biracial/multiracial, were portrayed as pitiful, "tragic mulattos," confused and rejected by people racialized as White and by those racialized as Black (Laszloffy and Rockquemore 2013).

In the post–civil rights era, more people began claiming a biracial/ multiracial identity (Korgen 1998). One of the most interesting aspects of the emergence of biracial/multiracial identities is that people started claiming this new racial identity despite lacking institutional support for such claims; for instance, the Census Bureau to this day does not offer a "biracial/multiracial" race category, despite demands from some groups to include such an option.

In the 1990s, a **multiracial movement** emerged in order to gain public recognition for the multiracial community, including a push for the inclusion of a multiracial category on the census. The multiracial movement combined several organizations under the umbrella organization the Association for Multiethnic Americans (AMEA), which sought to "identify and legally eliminate discrimination against multiracial individuals and families" (Williams 2006:1). Two other umbrella groups of multiracial Americans formed, Project RACE (Reclassify All Children Equally) and A Place For Us (APFU) (Williams 2006). While the groups differed, they all "shared the conviction that it was inaccurate and unacceptable to force multiracial Americans into monoracial categories" (Williams 2006:4). Civil rights groups were opposed to the addition of a multiracial category on the census, fearing a corresponding decline in minority populations as many people instead checked "biracial/multiracial." This would ultimately disadvantage minority communities since the census is used to determine need and the allocation of many government resources. The demand for a multiracial category was rejected by the Census Bureau; however, they did agree to allow people to "mark one or more" (MOOM) racial categories for the first time ever.

Many of the activists involved in the multiracial movement were parents racialized as White with children racialized as biracial/multiracial who argued that their children were being discriminated against due the denial of their multiraciality; specifically, their White ancestry was consistently disregarded by the lingering effects of the one-drop rule. Other scholars have argued that the discrimination biracial people face is not due to their biraciality but due to their Black ancestry; Black/White biracial people face the same discrimination as people racialized as Black face (Korgen 1998). Some critics of the multiracial movement argue that their goal was to provide their biracial/multiracial children with a higher status than Blacks; "the mere desire of white parents for their children to be identified as mixed-race (as opposed to black) signifies an implied acknowledgement that racial groups exist, that they exist in a hierarchy, and that separation from the subordinate group brings an individual closer to the dominant group" (Rockquemore and Brunsma 2002:14).While it is true that there is a racial hierarchy, it is also true that a significant part, the White ancestry, of a biracial/multiracial person's heritage has been denied by the ongoing social power of the one-drop rule.

Interestingly, a recent Pew Research Center 2015 study on multiracial individuals finds that 61 percent of people with a multiracial heritage do not identify as multiracial or mixed race, a phenomenon referred to as the **multiracial identity gap** (Goo 2015). The reasons for this vary; many say it is because they were raised as one race, and about as many say it is because of their phenotype—they look like a member of a particular race, which influences how others see them, and thus, it influences their racial identity. Others say it is because they did not know the family member who was of a different race. Additionally, about 30 percent of respondents in the

Pew Research Center's study on multiracial individuals say they have changed their racial identification over the course of their lifetimes, some moving from a monoracial identity to a multiracial identity, while others moved in the opposite direction (Goo 2015). This is a dramatic difference from most Americans who experience little to no fluidity in their racial identities over the course of their lifetime.

Toward a More Racially Just Society

Many scholars argue that the increasing presence of interracial relationships, multiracial families, and biracial/multiracial people is evidence we are moving toward a more racially just society (Cashin 2017; Kennedy 2003; Korgen 1998). As law professor Sheryll Cashin (2017:174) states, "I believe that we will reach a tipping point in race relations—a point when a critical mass of culturally dexterous whites accepts the loss of the centrality of whiteness. In other words, a critical mass of people not fragile and fearful of demographic change." Part of the argument is that this is evidence of decreasing racism, but a second argument is that the presence of Americans racialized as biracial/multiracial is evidence of the instability of the racial hierarchy itself (Korgen 1998).

Despite such hope, "interracial unions and multiracial children are no panacea for enduring problems of stratification" (Steinbugler 2012:xiii). The path to a more racially just society also relies on organizations, such as churches and social clubs, which must become multiracial (Yancey 2006). Research has found that people who attend multiracial churches are more likely to accept interracial marriage and are more likely to have racially heterogeneous social networks (Emerson, Kimbro, and Yancey 2002; Yancey 2001). We can look to the military for an example of how to successfully integrate an organization and its leadership, making multiraciality an organizational advantage (Moskos and Butler 1996; Yancey 2006).

Conclusion

In this chapter, we explore the ways race and racism manifest in the most intimate spheres of our lives—in our romantic relationships, our choice of marriage partners, family, and racial identity formation, emphasizing that until racism is confronted in this most intimate sphere of life, we will never become a racially just society.

Interracial relationships, from sexual relationships to marriage, were prohibited in over 41 states and territories between 1660 and 1967. All antimiscegenation laws prohibited Black–White interracial relationships, while sometimes restricting relationships between people racialized as White and people racialized as non-White. Such laws were not intended to prohibit racial minority group members from marrying each other but instead were designed to protect racial purity of people racialized as White by making interracial marriage with Whites illegal. By definition, then, as numbers of interracial relationships, multiracial families, and biracial/multiracial people increase, there remains hope that these changes can help pave the way toward a more racially just society.

KEY TERMS AND CONCEPTS ————————

Amalgamation 81

Antimiscegenation laws 82

Border patrolling 87

Boundary maintenance 87

Endogamous 84

Extended contact hypothesis 89

Formal social control 82

Informal social control 82

Marital assimilation 81

Multiracial identity gap 96

Multiracial movement 95

Racework 88

Rebound racism 87

Sexual racism 87

Social control 82

CRITICAL THINKING QUESTIONS ————————

1. Identify three interracial relationships in media and popular culture. How are these relationships framed? Does this fit with the research presented in this chapter? If not, speculate on why that is.

2. Since most scholarship on interracial relationships focuses on those racialized as Black–White, speculate on the applicability of the findings introduced in this chapter (specifically the section on navigating interracial relationships) to interracial relationships beyond Black–White.

3. Were you surprised by the data on interracial marriage? If so, were the rates lower than what you expected or higher? Think about why. What variables might make your perception of interracial relationships differ from the reality of the extent of them in the United States today?

RECOMMENDED READINGS ————————

Dalmage, Heather M. 2000. *Tripping on the Color Line: Black–White Multiracial Families in a Racially Divided World.* New Brunswick, NJ: Rutgers University Press.

Frankenberg, Ruth. 1993. *The Social Construction of Whiteness: White Women, Race Matters.* Minneapolis, MN: University of Minnesota Press.

Kennedy, Randall. 2003. *Interracial Intimacies: Sex, Marriage, Identity, and Adoption.* New York: Vintage Books Edition.

Korgen, Kathleen Odell. 1998. *From Black to Biracial: Transforming Racial Identity Among Americans.* Westport, CT: Praeger Publishers.

Rockquemore, Kerry Ann and David L. Brunsma. 2002. *Beyond Black: Biracial Identity in America.* Thousand Oaks, CA: SAGE.

Steinbugler, Amy C. 2012. *Beyond Loving: Intimate Racework in Lesbian, Gay, and Straight Interracial Relationships.* New York: Oxford University Press.

Yancey, George and Richard Lewis, Jr. 2009. *Interracial Families: Current Concepts and Controversies.* New York: Routledge.

CHAPTER 6

Race in a Global Context

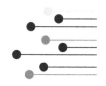

The colonial era (1500s to mid-1900s) marked the emergence of the concept of race, the hierarchical grouping of people based upon physical appearance (see Chapter 1). Race became an important social category in this era because in European colonizers' global explorations and quest for wealth and power, they encountered Indigenous peoples previously unknown to them. In their desire to exploit these new people and places for their own gain, European colonizers defined these Indigenous people as inferior; exploiting people is easier to justify when you dehumanize them, which was a key aspect of colonialism. **Colonialism** refers to a set of unequal relationships between colonizers and Indigenous people and the exploitation of the land, labor, and/or resources of the Indigenous people by the colonizer through violence. Colonial discourses revealed asymmetrical power relations found in the racial hierarchies that emerged out of colonialism and the slave trade. For instance, European colonizers described their relationship to Indigenous people as a "civilizing mission" and used metaphors of "darkness" and "primitiveness" repeatedly to describe the Indigenous peoples and cultures they encountered. They framed themselves as "civilized" and "superior" in comparison. Eventually, they racialized these identities.

With the implementation of the transatlantic slave trade, where Europeans forcibly took between 15 and 20 million Africans from their homes and enslaved them in the so-called New World between the fifteenth and the nineteenth centuries, the foundation of the Black–White racial hierarchy was established (Bennett 1966). While people have always voluntarily wandered, migrated, and explored lands far from their homeland, the four centuries of the transatlantic slave trade is the largest forced migration of people in world history. The descendants of the millions of people taken from West and Central Africa and enslaved in the Americas are referred to as the **African diaspora**. Scholars of the African diaspora focus on their agency and resistance, particularly their efforts to keep African traditions, cultures, and heritages alive despite being dispersed to all corners of the globe and being in cultures steeped in ideologies of anti-Blackness and White supremacy. Paul Gilroy (1993:39) emphasizes the common traits found among diasporic people racialized as Black, claiming "diasporic blacks share a memory of slavery, actively preserved as a living intellectual resource in their expressive political culture." Other scholars have challenged the centrality of slavery to the African diasporic experience (Golash-Boza 2011; Wright 2004). Nevertheless, "the concept of an African diaspora is not vacuous; the forced removal of millions of people from Africa clearly has left its mark on the world" (Golash-Boza 2011:7).

We began this book with the argument that race is a social construction, created during the colonial era; one of the pieces of evidence for that claim is that racial categories change across time and place. We have also emphasized the point that racial categorization systems are political and their creation and perpetuation is an exercise of power—meaning they are designed to meet the needs of the dominant group. Every country offers a different context out of which their racial hierarchies emerged, so what generalizations can be made about race across the globe? Sociologist Melissa Weiner (2012) offers a **critical global race theory** as a guide for understanding racial hierarchies across differing contexts, specifically identifying 10 indicators to determine whether and how racialization manifests in particular locations. These indicators include citizenship laws, state control of particular populations (what groups are surveilled and/or racially profiled), criminalization (what groups are more heavily policed), geographic segregation, socioeconomic status, and popular and political discourse, among others.

The United States' national narrative of itself as a "melting pot" and a "nation of immigrants" sometimes blinds us to the fact that most nations of the world are racially and ethnically diverse; it is not something unique to the United States. Racial diversity in the Western hemisphere began with the arrival of European colonizers to countries already inhabited by millions of Indigenous peoples and the importation of millions of Africans forced into servitude, while European racial diversity is more recent, the bulk of which is a result of immigration from former African and Asian colonies in the postcolonial and post–World War II era.

This chapter will explore how race varies across cultures, from who is racialized as Black, White, Brown, or Indigenous, to how racial understandings inform social policies, to the ways racial inequality and White supremacy manifest globally. We begin by exploring race and global White supremacy in Latin America, South Africa, contemporary Europe, and Australia. We conclude with a path toward a more racially just society with coverage of reparations and racial reconciliation projects as a way to understand how individuals and nations can heal from centuries of racism. Importantly, if race, racism, and White supremacy are global, so is resistance to racism, as the global protests in support of Black Lives Matter in the spring and summer of 2020 exemplify.

Race in Latin America

Most Latin American countries have a multiracial history that is at least superficially similar to that of the United States, with people of Indigenous,

African, and European descent making up the bulk of their populations. However, Latin America experienced higher rates of interracial mixing over the centuries than did the U.S., primarily because their European colonizers were Spain and Portugal, countries that did not send as many people to the so-called "New World" during the colonial period. Despite this, throughout Latin America, one still finds racial hierarchies. Princeton sociologist Edward Telles (2014:1) sums it up best by saying, "Social distinctions and ethnic hierarchies based on phenotype, ancestry, and language have been prominent features of social life throughout the Western Hemisphere for more than five hundred years" as a result of European colonization. While each Latin American country has its own specific cultural and historical context that created their current **racial order**, a term that refers to the hierarchical ordering of groups on the basis of their physical characteristics and the beliefs and practices that support that ordering, it is beyond the scope of this text to explore each in depth (Hochschild, Weaver, and Burch 2012). Instead, we are going to focus on three broad themes that are pervasive throughout the region. These include an explicit embrace of racial and cultural mixing, referred to as *mestizaje*, or mestizos, inequality and colorism, and the erasure of Blackness. While we will discuss these separately, they are interrelated concepts.

Mestizaje

Telles (2014) argues that today, most Latin American countries have constitutionally embraced multiculturalism. This embrace includes a recognition of the discrimination and inequality faced by citizens with Indigenous and African ancestries, which is a shift away from previous eras (Telles 2014). In previous eras, some Latin American countries at different points in their histories proudly boasted of their mixed-race, mestizo heritage and declared themselves free from racism, despite simultaneously attempting to erase Blackness from their national narrative (Pinho 2009; Sue 2013; Telles 2004). In both Mexico and Brazil, the embrace of their mestizo heritage was used as evidence that they were a **racial democracy**, which currently refers to a country where all racial groups can participate in the democratic process and hold at least some political power; initially, Brazilian scholars used the term to refer to a country that had harmonious race relations (Freyre 1933; Omi and Winant 1994).

Mexico claimed the mantle of a racial democracy in the early twentieth century, after the Mexican Revolution, by promoting the idea of *mestizaje* to unify the country and erase the old racial hierarchies (Wade 2017). Specifically, the idea of race mixture was "linked to progress, equality, and modernity" (Wade 2017:9). Importantly, this claim challenged dominant European and American views at the time, which embraced scientific racism, eugenics, and ideas of racial purity. A key aspect of Western racist ideology was that "racial mixing lowers biological quality" (Davis 1991:25). Mexican elites instead reframed race mixture positively, arguing that mestizo represented "a culturally and biologically superior race" (Sue 2013:15). This reframing results in the racialization of Mexicans around the idea that a real Mexican was mestizo (Sue 2013). Additionally, these claims were essential to global political jockeying, as the Mexican government "used claims that the country was a racial democracy as a way of taking the moral high ground in relation to the United States and its racially segregated society" (Wade 2017:10).

This history of the qualified embrace of mestizo manifests today in at least two ways. One is in terms of identity construction and the second relates to attitudes toward interracial relationships. The racialization of Mexicans as mestizo and the simultaneous cultural veneration of Whiteness, discussed later, results in dark-skinned Mexicans having to navigate their identity between their stigmatized dark skin and their national identities, which, as mestizo, shows they clearly belong. Mexicans racialized as White also carefully navigate this color-nationality terrain through different strategies, such as downplaying their Whiteness and proclaiming their loyalty to Mexico. The national ideology of *mestizaje* becomes a key aspect of identity for groups yet is navigated differently depending on one's skin color (Sue 2013).

In theory, one would assume that a culture that embraces *mestizaje* would not have an issue with interracial relationships, but research finds that Mexicans do not embrace such relationships unconditionally. Opposition to relationships with people who are darker-skinned is common in Mexico; opponents use the language of "personal preference" for lighter-skinned individuals, justifying this preference that runs counter to their national ideology by emphasizing the desire to "lighten" their children. There is a widespread preference for babies to be born light-skinned and with green or blue eyes; thus, marrying light-skinned or people racialized as White is favored (Sue 2013). Research finds that "anticipation about a baby's color is most intense within families where members are noticeably different colors. Under these circumstances, individuals perceive a wide range of possible outcomes for newborns in the game of genetic roulette" (Sue 2013:74).

Similarly, Brazil embraced race mixing, even to the point of arguing proudly that they are the most racially mixed nation in the world. Scholar Gilberto Freyre (1933) was an early proponent of the idea that high rates of miscegenation implied something positive about Brazilian race relations, a signal that there was little to no racism to be found in the country. Throughout the twentieth century, race mixture was the foundation of Brazilian national character (Telles 2014). During the 1930s, the Brazilian government started to embrace their multiracial heritage. One way this played out was to end the restrictions on cultural expressions that had distinctly African origins—particularly the samba (dance) and capoeira (an Afro-Brazilian martial art).

This historical embrace of race mixture informs Brazil's current racial classification system and Brazilian individuals' racial identity claims, unsurprisingly. For instance, racial categories in Brazil have long been contested, thus, difficult to study. The Project on Ethnicity and Race in Latin America (PERLA) included several ways for respondents to describe their race (Telles 2014). The first was an open-ended question, the second was self-identification from a list of choices, and the third involved having the interviewer classify the person's race based upon their appearance. This strategy resulted in the percentage of Blacks shifting from 6 percent who self-identified as Black to 59.4 percent who interviewers classified as Black or Brown (Telles 2014). Today, 43 percent of Brazilians identify as mixed race, and 30 percent who identify as White have some African ancestry (De Oliveira 2017). In Brazil, an individual's racial classification can change over time, as well, which is not generally true in the U.S., where racial classification tends to be stable over the course of one's life (Gullickson and Torche 2014).

While Brazil has a high rate of interracial marriage, at least 20 times the rate in the United States, there is still evidence of the privileging of Whiteness (Telles 2004). For instance, some research finds that marriage is viewed as one path toward "Whitening." Similar to Mexico, research finds that in Brazil, marrying White is viewed as a path of social mobility for one's children (Degler 1971; Telles 2004). Sociologists use the concept of **status exchange** to suggest that individuals in heterogamous (meaning mixed on any number of status variables, such as race, class, or educational status) marriages trade status characteristics. In other words, a person racialized as a racial minority with high educational attainment can be seen as engaging in a status exchange if they marry a person racialized as White; their (high) educational status compensated for their (low) racial status, and they were able to "marry up." Scholars studying status exchange and marriage in Brazil found that despite the more fluid racial boundaries there, this was a pattern (Gullickson and Torche 2014). Importantly, since the emergence of Black consciousness and the implementation of race-based social policies in Brazil, which began in 2001, individuals in interracial relationships are more likely to be offended by the idea of Whitening, even when those around them still think of their marriage as being about Whitening, discussed later (Osuji 2013).

Colorism and Inequality

Throughout Latin America, despite variation in racial categorization systems and an embrace of race mixing, racism, anti-Blackness, and racial inequality are persistent. Throughout Latin America, lighter-skinned people are advantaged and hold higher status, and darker-skinned people, those with more African features, face discrimination and inequality. Due to these patterns, Latin American countries are referred to as **pigmentocracies**, countries where skin color rather than ancestry is the key determinant of social stratification (Lipschutz 1944; Telles 2014). This is also known as colorism, or discrimination based upon skin color rather than on one's racial category or ancestry (see Chapter 1).

In places like Mexico and Brazil, colorism is also cultural. Brazilians are less likely to use the term *race* to define themselves or others in everyday speech, even though the census has official racial categories. Regardless of the racial groups they belong to, across Latin America, "light-skinned people, regardless of their identity, had higher levels of education and higher occupational status than their darker counterparts" (Telles 2014:226). The pigmentocracy in Latin America is a remnant of their colonial past (Sue 2013). In Brazil, Mexico, Colombia, and Peru, persons with lighter skin were the most advantaged, from the likelihood that they would obtain a university education to whether they were in white-collar occupations, domestic workers, or peasants (see Table 6.1 from Telles 2014; full reference is at the end of the chapter).

However, when it comes to racial classifications, there is more variation than one would expect (colorism being distinct from racial categorization). According to PERLA findings, in Mexico, Colombia, and Peru, people racialized as White were not always the dominant group; mestizos sometimes had higher social status than people racialized as White. Also, people who identify as pardo (Brown) and preto (Black) in Brazil, according to census racial categories, are equally disadvantaged. Finally, individuals who self-identify as Indigenous in Mexico, Peru, and Colombia consistently ranked lowest on socioeconomic status (Telles 2014).

Current scholars who study inequality in Brazil focus less on race mixing and more on **social exclusion**, the lack of social integration of particular groups or persons and their lack of access to resources or limits on their citizenship rights (Telles 2004). Brazil is one of the most

Table 6.1 Inequality by Country and Color Group (%)

	Light (1–3)	Medium (4–5)	Dark (6+)
With university education (excluding students)			
Brazil	22	14	6
Colombia	20	15	13
Mexico	11	4	4
Peru	26	18	15
With primary education (excluding students)			
Brazil	29	31	39
Colombia	20	31	31
Mexico	55	66	73
Peru	14	17	22
In white-collar occupations			
Brazil	30	26	23
Colombia	28	23	26
Mexico	36	28	18
Peru	39	34	31
Domestic worker, farmer, or peasant			
Brazil	13	16	24
Colombia	29	42	35
Mexico	24	36	49
Peru	7	10	12

Source: Telles, Edward. 2014. *Pigmentocracies: Ethnicity, Race, and Color in Latin America.* Chapel Hill, NC: University of North Carolina Press.

unequal societies in the world, with approximately one-third of its population living in poverty, and Black and Brown people are most likely to be in poverty (Telles 2004). According to the World Bank, Brazil currently ranks eighth in terms of countries with the greatest inequality out of 150 countries.

Whitening and the Erasure of Blackness

In the early twentieth century, many Latin American countries, including Mexico, Brazil, Peru, Venezuela, and Colombia, engaged in explicit **Whitening strategies** aimed at increasing the percentages of people racialized as White. These were explicitly political moves in that elites throughout Latin America were concerned that their large population of Black and Indigenous people hindered their national development. Many Latin American elites "believed that only Europeans were capable of achieving full progress and that their large nonwhite populations would doom them to perpetual second-class status. . . . To be modern like Europe and the United States, they thought that a white population was essential" (Telles 2014:17).

Efforts to erase Blackness began immediately after the end of slavery in Brazil in 1888 (De Oliveira 2017). By the early 1900s, Brazilian scholars proposed Whitening strategies that were in line with eugenicist thinking of the era. These strategies included encouraging miscegenation between people racialized as White and non-Whites. It was believed that White genes were dominant and, combined with higher White fertility rates, this strategy could result in a White or mostly White population in one generation (Telles 2004). Policy makers in Brazil also established immigration policies designed to Whiten the population. For instance, they sought immigrants from Europe by recruiting heavily and subsidizing their immigration, while simultaneously restricting Asian immigration until 1910. Behavioral Whitening strategies were implemented in the 1930s, which included embracing diets, education, health, and hygiene habits linked to people racialized as White and rejecting cultural practices associated with African or Indigenous cultures (Pinho 2009). The idea behind these Whitening strategies was to eliminate the population of people racialized as Black, under the assumption that Blacks were inferior.

Whitening in Brazil was also about class mobility. The idea that social mobility leads to cultural mobility, that "money whitens," is part of Brazil's national narrative (Bailey, Loveman, and Muiz 2012). This demographic pattern is described by scholars as the **mulatto escape hatch**, acknowledging that in the Brazilian racial hierarchy, people racialized as Brown exist on an intermediate strata, between those racialized as White, who are at the top, and those racialized as Black, who are at the bottom (Degler 1971).

Anti-Blackness was so pervasive that throughout Latin America, people racialized as Black and Indigenous have had to mobilize and demand justice and recognition, including on national censuses (Telles 2014).

Research finds that in Peru, Blacks experience considerable racism, including being "stereotypically displayed on television, in the newspaper, and on billboards as cooks, as primitive, as hypersexual, and as unintelligent. In addition, there are common jokes that associate blacks with criminality" (Golash-Boza 2011:192–193). Current research on race and disparity in Brazil finds that "blackness per se—as opposed to gradations of nonwhiteness—bears a distinct negative cost in Brazil. The specific disadvantages faced by individuals who others see not as 'brown' or 'nonwhite'" (Bailey, Loveman, and Muiz 2012:116).

Evidence that anti-Blackness remains alive and well in Brazil can be found in the election of Jair Bolsonaro to the presidency in 2018. He campaigned on and upon election made good on promises to roll back affirmative action policies that have been designed to help Afro-Brazilians. Indeed, "fomenting antiblackness was critical to Bolsonaro's election" (da Silva and Larkins 2019). There has been a documented increase in blatant racial hatred since his election, including a Black female sociology professor in São Paulo who was harassed with a swastika on the classroom chalkboard and the words "negro damn whore" written under it (da Silva and Larkins 2019).

South Africa

When we think of race and South Africa, apartheid comes to mind; apartheid was a legal system of racial segregation and institutionalized inequality in place from 1948 to 1994. However, even before the country implemented formal apartheid, colonial powers had dominated South Africa for five centuries (Knaus and Brown 2016). Under apartheid, every aspect of life was dictated by "race laws" designed to maintain the supremacy of people racialized as White and the subordination of people racialized as Black. Somewhat similar to the United States' approach to Jim Crow era race relations, which had segregation at its core, people racialized as White in South Africa established an elaborate system of segregation and discrimination known as apartheid. Continued dominance of people racialized as White in South Africa remains particularly insidious; as of 2011, people racialized as White composed only 8 percent of the population, while those racialized as Black Africans composed 80 percent, people racialized as Coloured composed 9 percent, those racialized as Indian or Asian composed 2 percent, and 1 percent were classified as other. In other words, "South

Africa is a nation-state in which 8% of the population exercises power and privilege over 92% of the population" (Knaus and Brown 2016:11).

Under apartheid, interracial marriage and interracial sex were illegal. Comedian Trevor Noah (2016), born to a Xhosa mother racialized as Black and a Swiss father racialized as White at a time when such a relationship was punishable by five years in prison, described himself as "born a crime." Strict residential segregation was implemented, with people racialized as Black being forced into separate townships, then eventually to Bantustans, separate homelands; the homelands policy resulted in the forced relocation of an estimated 3.5 million people between 1960 and 1983 (Worden 2007). In addition to residential segregation, social segregation extended to all amenities, from public transportation to cinemas, restaurants, schools, and sports facilities. Since people racialized as Black were needed to work in White areas, they were required to carry a passbook, which was updated monthly with their employer's signature, noting their right to be in the White area. People racialized as White held all the political power, as well. Finally, opposition to apartheid was considered a violation of the Suppression of Communism Act (1950) and could result in a person being "banned." To be banned meant that it was illegal to publish their image or broadcast their words; a person became *personae non gratae* under a ban. This meant that most South Africans had no idea what antiapartheid activists looked like unless they knew them personally. Despite this—and the brutality, violence, and oppression of apartheid overall—people racialized as Black did protest their subordination. This led to an expansion of police forces and an increase in extreme, violent state repression (Worden 2007).

Black resistance to apartheid, coupled with international pressure, condemnation, and disinvestment, eventually resulted its dismantling beginning in 1990. It began with the repeal of key aspects of apartheid, including unbanning antiapartheid political leaders, releasing political prisoners, and eventually allowing the first fully democratic elections to occur. A Black South African activist, Nelson Mandela, who had been incarcerated for 27 years for his antiapartheid political activism, won the presidency in 1994, signaling an end to formal apartheid. Under Mandela, the new government approved a constitution that was one of the most liberal in the world and forbade discrimination along the lines of race, gender, language, or religion (Worden 2007).

Despite the progressive constitution, today South Africa is the most unequal society in the world, according to the Organization for Economic Cooperation and Development (OECD), with a GINI index of 62 (where 0 represents perfect equality, 100 perfect inequality, better thought of as extreme inequality) (Suneson and Stebbins 2019). This inequality is also racialized; the bottom 60 percent of the population, almost all of whom are racialized as Black, control only 7 percent of the nation's wealth (Baker 2019). While the demise of apartheid brought about a slow-growing, small Black middle class and a small, uber-wealthy Black elite, the lives of most Black people have not changed very dramatically in terms of their material conditions (Baker 2019). People of Color are overwhelmingly impoverished, unemployed, undereducated, and incarcerated; "these extremes are colonialism's and apartheid's legacy; centuries of grand inequity left a sea of poverty and crime in its wake" (Dreisinger 2016:60).

Schools in postapartheid South Africa are "unequal, segregated, and differentially staffed" (Knaus and Brown 2016:28). Schools populated predominantly by students racialized as Black and "Coloured" receive only one-tenth the funding of schools with students racialized as White and are overcrowded and underresourced. Research finds that Whiteness is a permanent feature of schools in South Africa and that schools are "locations where the rules of race are taught and reinforced . . . [and] are designed to maintain a permanent undereducated workforce" (Knaus and Brown 2016:16).

In addition to racial disparities in matriculation rates (similar to high school graduation rates in the U.S.) and standardized test scores, disparities in educational infrastructure are profound, extending even to unequal access to toilets. For instance,

> in primary schools, learners at predominantly Black schools had minimal access to toilets and averaged 140 learners per toilet, more than twice that of Coloured schools (65 learners per toilet), and more than five times that of White schools (26 learners per toilet). . . . For learners at Black and Coloured schools, toilet wait times increase significantly as they age or ascend to higher levels of schooling. (Knaus and Brown 2016:69)

Global White Supremacy: Australia and Contemporary Europe

While racial categorizations can and do vary, and countries differ in their official acknowledgment of race, racial hierarchies and inequality are defining features of the modern world. For that reason, we shift our discussion to global White supremacy, specifically exploring its manifestation in Australia and contemporary Europe. **Global White supremacy** refers to a "historically based and institutionally perpetuated system of exploitation and oppression of continents, nations, and peoples classified as non-white" by continents, nations, and peoples that classify themselves as White (Blay 2011:6). This system exists in order to maintain White wealth, power, and privilege. Whiteness, like race in general, is socially constructed (see Chapter 1). Whiteness is also constructed globally. Scholars argue that in the late nineteenth and early twentieth centuries, countries like South Africa, Australia, and the United States worked in solidarity to create "White men's nations"; essentially, Whiteness became "the basis of geopolitical alliances and a subjective sense of self" (Lake and Reynolds 2008:3). This was done through the transnational circulation of ideas and strategies of exclusion, deportation, and segregation and through the use of state surveillance of the population through passports, the census, and literacy tests (Lake and Reynolds 2008).

Some countries implemented explicit Whitening policies, as previous examples from Latin America exemplify. Others established immigration policies that intentionally privileged Whiteness. Australia did both with the implementation of the Immigration Restriction Act, which became known as the *White Australia* policies. Under these policies, thousands of Pacific Islanders were expelled from Australia, and immigration restrictions on non-Whites were implemented, essentially amounting to racial segregation on a global scale (Lake and Reynolds 2008). Through these efforts, Australian elites racialized as White were consciously attempting to align themselves with the nations of the world that were racialized as White, such as Great Britain and the United States, rather than with their Asian neighbors (Jones 2003). The Japanese were vocal in their critique of these policies; they were not as offended that Australia was attempting to ban people racialized as non-White as they were offended that they had been included in the category of non-White (Lake and Reynolds 2008).

Many Australians express embarrassment over this history. As of 2019, almost 21 percent of Australia's population are of non-European heritage, and 3 percent are Indigenous (Soutphommasane 2019). Much like Europe, discussed next, Australia witnessed massive immigration in the post–World War II era, to the point that today, almost half of the population is either immigrant or the children of immigrants. And yet, the idea of who is a real Australian is still linked to Whiteness. Essentially, "whiteness in Australia involves a hierarchy of belonging . . . whiteness matters. It shapes how we talk about issues, and who has the right to talk with authority . . . it frequently leaves racial minorities as passive players in public debates" (Soutphommasane 2019).

Race in Contemporary Europe

Contemporary European countries are mostly silent about race, racism, and Whiteness. One's first thought concerning race and racism in Europe likely turns to the Holocaust. Due to that intellectual linkage, perhaps unsurprisingly, "For Europeans, race is not, or really is no longer. European racial denial concerns wanting race in the wake of World War II categorically to implode, to erase itself" (Goldberg 2006:334). Scholar David Theo Goldberg (2006) speaks of racial projects as regional, as being culturally embedded. He introduces the idea of **racial Europeanization**, which refers to the European denial of and failure to acknowledge race and racism, "rendering race unmentionable, unspeakable if not as a reference to an anti-Semitism of the past" (Goldberg 2006:339). Since the word *race* is linked to the Holocaust, it is considered taboo in many places in Europe.

In the case of France, this silence on race is official; France has enshrined colorblindness into law and policy. For instance, France bans collecting statistics along racial and ethnic lines; thus, there are no race or ethnicity questions on the census, nor do federal or state agencies keep track of racial data. A company cannot recruit job applicants racialized as racial minorities or establish training programs that target racial minorities. The word *race* was recently removed from the French constitution (Beaman 2018; Bleich 2003). The reason for this official stance of colorblindness is that all individuals are supposed to be French; racial/ethnic differences should be irrelevant.

Despite this official policy of colorblindness, France is still a society where Whiteness is the norm, the default (Beaman 2019). Specifically, Whiteness and belonging—Whiteness and citizenship—are linked. Research by Jean Beaman on second-generation North African French middle-class citizens finds their continued marginalization and outsider status due to their race/ethnicity. These people perceive themselves as doing everything right; they are educated, upwardly mobile professionals, and they embrace French society and culture. Yet they still experience discrimination, from constant assumptions that they are foreigners rather than citizens to racial stereotypes that they should be feared and are not to be trusted (Beaman 2017). In addition to Whiteness being the default, French people use the terms *Muslim, foreigners,* or *immigrants* to describe non-Whites, even though these terms are inaccurate descriptions of the bulk of People of Color in France (Beaman 2018).

We can see racial Europeanization at work in Switzerland, too. There is the general belief among the Swiss that there is no racism in Switzerland.

This understanding comes from the conflation of race with immigrants found throughout Europe. Switzerland's lack of a colonial past, which makes them distinct from France, the UK, Germany, and the Netherlands, means they do not have a significant immigrant population from their former colonies. Much like in France, non-White immigrants in Switzerland are racialized as "others," yet they simultaneously deny the existence of racism there. Denying racism and embracing the attitude of racelessness is part of the assimilation process for non-White immigrants, part of becoming incorporated into their adopted country (Cretton 2018).

The idea of racial Europeanization is alive and well in the Netherlands, as well. Using the word *race* is taboo, "to be referred to indirectly (as in, 'she is dark') but not in terms of political, social or even statistical belonging (as in: 'white voters'). In the Netherlands, it is considered morally wrong to register according to 'race'" (Essed and Trienekens 2008:52). Yet the familiar critique of immigrants is widespread, particularly the accusation that they are incapable of assimilating into Dutch society. White skin is also essential to a sense of belonging in Dutch society (Essed and Trienekens 2008).

Toward a More Racially Just Society

Many countries across the globe have embraced racial justice efforts, such as racial reconciliation projects, restorative justice, and reparations, in order to heal racial injustices. We are going to briefly introduce three examples of reconciliation projects here: the South African Truth and Reconciliation Commission, Rwandan reconciliation through *gacaca* courts, and the campaign for reparations in the United States. Sociologist Alondra Nelson (2016) defines **reconciliation projects** as efforts to generate acknowledgment of a social injury, campaigns for state apologies, and public deliberations about racial history and events, all with an eye on healing past and ongoing racial injustices.

Some of these reconciliation projects approach the problem through the lens of **restorative justice**, which is "a theory of justice that emphasizes repairing the harm caused by criminal behavior. It is best accomplished through cooperative processes that allow all willing stakeholders to meet . . . this can lead to transformation of people, relationships and communities" ("Lesson 1" n.d.). In the restorative justice framework, healing happens through dialogue rather than punishment, with the active participation of victims. Victims require four things: "truthful answers; empowerment; restoration of respect, usually achieved by the repeated telling of stories of harm; and restitution, which can be a statement of responsibility or a literal payback" (Dreisinger 2016:82). While this might seem hard to believe that such a simple process of honest dialogue can heal deep racial wounds, there is some evidence that "an honest interpersonal/interracial dialogue about racism and reconciliation, when made public, can open up new potential for growth in racial understanding, repentance, and healing—especially among Whites, who react defensively to more monologic discourse about the pervasiveness of racism and white guilt" (Hatch 2016:95).

After the dismantling of apartheid, a Truth and Reconciliation Commission was established in South Africa in 1995. The idea was that South Africa could only move forward, that reconciliation could only happen, if everyone knew the truth about what happened under apartheid. Thus, in exchange for amnesty, "full and public testimony by individuals and political parties about actions for which they were responsible" was required (Worden 2007:163). These public confessions unearthed the extent of violence and brutality that occurred, including the murder of Black activist Steve Biko, but also the brutality directed at thousands of lesser-known, everyday South Africans racialized as Black. Part of a reconciliation project involves making reparations, and these were initially part of South Africa's plan. However, "long after the TRC had completed its work, reparations to victims and their families were still unpaid" (Worden 2007:163).

A more effective example of a reconciliation project involved the *gacaca* courts in Rwanda, used as a way to heal from the genocide that occurred in 1994. The Rwandan genocide was particularly violent and brutal. An estimated one million Tutsis were slaughtered, many with machetes, by the Hutus in a 100-day period. These were neighbors killing neighbors. Tutsi women were taken as sex slaves and raped. The brutality of the situation is hard to comprehend. And yet, survivors and perpetrators of this massacre are alive today and are working to heal (Dreisinger 2016).

Rwandans decided that with the high numbers of perpetrators, sending them to prison was not a realistic option. They started off doing that, but prisons were soon overcrowded and disease-ridden (the extent of the overcrowding is also hard to fathom; spaces built for 12,000 prisoners held 130,000) ("Justice Compromised" 2011). Criminal courts were also moving far too slowly to address the massive numbers of perpetrators. Rwandans decided these cases would be handled by traditional Rwandan courts known as gacaca courts, which normally handled community conflicts, designed to promote communal healing and rebuilding. They put a focus on the truth, reconciliation, and national unity. Perpetrators of this violence had to engage in reparations—they had to give back to their community, in addition to telling the truth in court, in exchange for amnesty. Rwanda's "experiment in mass community-based justice has been a mixed success" ("Justice Compromised" 2011).

In the United States, there has been a long-standing campaign for **reparations**, some compensation and an official apology to former slaves or the descendants of slaves as a way to right the wrong and to repair the wounds caused by 250 years of slavery, another 100 years of Jim Crow, decades of mass incarceration, and the entire history of social and economic injury people racialized as Black have suffered due to American racism. This is not a new idea. Reparations to former slaves or descendants of slaves was first proposed in the 1880s by Walter Vaughan, a Southerner racialized as White (Blight 2006). Bills have been introduced in Congress since 1890 to provide reparations, and congressional representative John Conyers introduced a bill to establish a committee to study the effects of slavery every year since 1989; yet the bill never made it out of committee hearings. However, on June 19, 2019, the House of Representatives held the first meeting to finally consider the bill to study the effects of slavery and to consider a national apology for the harm it caused. This is the first time reparations for people racialized as Black have been discussed in the nation's capital. Scholar William A. Darity Jr., a leading expert on reparations, said, "To be blunt, I am more optimistic than I have ever been in my life about the prospect of the enactment of a reparations program that is comprehensive and transformative" (Stolberg 2019).

There is considerable precedent for reparations. Germany paid reparations to individual Jews and to the state of Israel for the Holocaust; South Africa's Truth and Reconciliation Committee included reparations, although they were never actually paid; and the United States paid reparations to Japanese Americans interned during World War II or their descendants. African American public intellectual Ta-Nehisi Coates (2014) wrote an essay on reparations in the *Atlantic*, which is credited with reviving attention toward the issue today. Reparations for Americans racialized as Black is only the beginning, however. Reparations need to include people racialized as Native American and other groups racialized as non-White for the historic and current harm they suffer due to racism.

Conclusion

This chapter has broadly explored the ways anti-Blackness and a privileging of Whiteness manifest across the globe, and the rest of the text investigated the ways race, racism, and privilege operate in the United States. One piece of evidence that shows that race is a social construction is the fact that understandings of race and racial categorization systems vary cross-culturally. If race were a biological category, culture would not matter.

Despite such cross-cultural variations, modern societies are characterized by racial hierarchies, with some people racialized as Black and existing on the margins of society and other people racialized as White reaping unearned benefits. White privilege is global due to the presence of global White supremacy.

Despite centuries of White dominance, I do not want to end this book implying that status hierarchies are static, unchanging. When we say that race is a social construction, a liberating idea is embedded in that concept: that it can be deconstructed. Status hierarchies are always being negotiated, altered, and transformed, often due to obvious external forces, like social movement activism. Reconciliation projects, restorative justice, and reparations are evidence that we can heal and move forward from the global scourge of racism. And the global racial justice protests triggered by the killing of George Floyd by a Minneapolis police officer have inspired changes that many of us thought we would never see, including the removal of Confederate monuments throughout the South, the end of the use of racialized images in advertising like Aunt Jemima, and the end of the use of a racial slur, the "Redskins," as the name for an NFL team located in the nation's capital. More changes are needed, of course. And those will take work. In that spirit, I end this book with an inspirational quote by one of the most prominent U.S. social justice activists, who passed in July 2020 after a lifetime of fighting for what was right, Representative John Lewis (1940–2020):

> Do not get lost in a sea of despair. Be hopeful, be optimistic. Our struggle is not the struggle of a day, a week, a month, or a year, it is the struggle of a lifetime. Never, ever be afraid to make some noise and get in good trouble, necessary trouble.

KEY TERMS AND CONCEPTS ———

CRITICAL THINKING QUESTIONS

1. Consider the regional and global racial patterns explored in this chapter, including global White supremacy, Latin American pigmentocracies, and racial Europeanization. To what extent do these reflect global inequalities—wealthy nations of the global North and poor nations of the global South. In other words, explain how the global racial hierarchy may be connected to the global economic or class hierarchy.

2. When considering global racial patterns, do you see evidence of increasing antiracism or evidence of increasing racism? Support your answer. To what extent is racial justice possible nationally, regionally, or globally? Explain your answer.

3. What do you think of France's official colorblind strategy? What are the strengths of such an approach? The weaknesses? How does this differ from the unofficial colorblindness in the U.S., where colorblindness is the norm but not official?

RECOMMENDED READINGS

Beaman, Jean. 2017. *Citizen Outsider: Children of North African Immigrants in France.* Berkeley, CA: University of California Press.

Lake, Marilyn and Henry Reynolds. 2008. *Drawing the Global Colour Line: White Men's Countries and the International Challenges of Racial Equality.* Cambridge, UK: Cambridge University Press.

Sue, Christina. 2013. *Land of the Cosmic Race: Race Mixture, Racism, and Blackness in Mexico.* New York: Oxford University Press.

Telles, Edward. 2004. *Race in Another America: The Significance of Skin Color in Brazil.* Princeton, NJ: Princeton University Press.

Telles, Edward. 2014. *Pigmentocracies: Ethnicity, Race, and Color in Latin America.* Chapel Hill, NC: University of North Carolina Press.

References

Alba, Richard and Victor Nee. 2003. *Remaking the American Mainstream: Assimilation and Contemporary Immigration.* Cambridge, MA: Harvard University Press.

Alexander, Michelle. 2010. *The New Jim Crow: Mass Incarceration in the Age of Colorblindness.* New York: The New Press.

Aliprantis, Dionissi and Daniel Carroll. 2019. "What Is Behind the Persistence of the Racial Wealth Gap?" *Economic Commentary Federal Reserve Bank of Cleveland* Issue Feb. 3:1–6.

Allport, Gordon. 1954. *The Nature of Prejudice.* Boston, MA: Addison-Wesley Press.

Altonji, Joseph G. and Ulrich Doraszelski. 2005. "The Role of Permanent Income and Demographics in Black/White Differences in Wealth." *Journal of Human Resources* 60(1):1–30.

American Civil Liberties Union. 2014. "War Comes Home: The Excessive Militarization of American Policing." New York: ACLU.

Anderson, Tre'Vell. 2017. "4 Latino Stereotypes in TV and Film That Need to Go." *Los Angeles Times* April 27. Retrieved July 3, 2020 (https://www.latimes.com/entertainment/movies/la-et-mn-latino-stereotypes-20170428-htmlstory.html).

"Anti-Semitic Stereotypes Persist in America, Survey Shows." 2020. *ADL* Jan. 29. Retrieved July 5, 2020 (https://www.adl.org/news/press-releases/anti-semitic-stereotypes-persist-in-america-survey-shows).

Armenta, Amada. 2018. "Racializing Crimmigration: Structural Racism, Colorblindness, and the Institutional Production of Immigrant Criminality." *Sociology of Race and Ethnicity* 3(1):82–95.

Azzarito, Laura and Lewis Harrison, Jr. 2008. "White Men Can't Jump: Race, Gender, and Natural Athleticism." *International Review for Sociology of Sport* 43(4):347–64.

Bailey, Stanley R., Mara Loveman, and Jeronimo O. Muiz. 2013. "Measures of 'Race' and the Analysis of Racial Inequality in Brazil." *Social Science Research* 429(1):106–19.

Baker, Aryn. 2019. "What South Africa Can Teach Us as Worldwide Inequality Grows." *Time* May 2. Retrieved June 14, 2020 (https://time.com/longform/south-africa-unequal-country).

Ballantine, Summer. 2019. "Black Missouri Drivers 91% More Likely to Be Stopped, State Attorney General Finds." *PBS News Hour* June 10. Retrieved June 11, 2020 (https://www.pbs.org/newshour/nation/black-missouri-drivers-91-more-likely-to-be-stopped-state-attorney-general-finds).

Barsky, Robert, John Bound, Kerwin Ko Charles, and Joseph P. Lupton. 2002. "Accounting for the Black–White Wealth Gap: A Nonparametic Approach." *Journal of the American Statistical Association* 97(459):663–73.

Bazelon, Emily. 2020. "A Discussion About How to Reform Policing." *New York Times Magazine* June 13, 2020. Retrieved Sept. 22, 2020 (https://www.nytimes.com/interactive/2020/06/13/magazine/police-reform.html).

Beaman, Jean. 2017. *Citizen Outsider: Children of North African Immigrants in France.* Berkeley: University of California Press.

Beaman, Jean. 2018. "Feeling Race When Race Does Not 'Exist.'" *UC Press Blog* Aug. 12. Retrieved June 11, 2020 (https://www.ucpress.edu/blog/37799/feeling-race-when-race-does-not-exist).

Beaman, Jean. 2019. "A French People White? Toward an Understanding of Whiteness in Republican France." *Identities: Global Studies in Culture and Power* 26(5):546–62.

Bedi, Sonu. 2014. "Sexual Racism: Intimacy as a Matter of Justice." *The Journal of Politics* 77(4):998–1011.

Bennett, Lerone, Jr. 1966. *Before the Mayflower: A History of the Negro in America 1619–1964.* Baltimore, MD: Penguin.

Berg, Charles Ramírez. 2002. *Latino Images in Film: Stereotypes, Subversion, and Resistance.* Austin: University of Texas Press.

Bertrand, Marianne and Sendhill Mullainathan. 2004. "Are Emily and Greg More Employable Than Lakisha and Jamal? A Field Experiment on Labor Market Discrimination." *The American Economic Review* 94(4):991–1013.

Bialik, Kristen. 2017. "Key Facts About Race and Marriage, 50 Years After *Loving v. Virginia.*" *Pew Research Center* June 12. Retrieved June 10, 2020 (https://www.pewresearch.org/fact-tank/2017/06/12/key-facts-about-race-and-marriage-50-years-after-loving-v-virginia).

Blackwell, Debra L. and Daniel T. Lichtner. 2004. "Homogamy Among Dating, Cohabiting, and Married Couples." *The Sociological Quarterly* 45(4):719–37.

Blau, Francine D. and John W. Graham. 1990. "Black–White Differences in Asset Composition." *The Quarterly Journal of Economics* 105(2):321–39.

Blay, Yabba Amgborale. 2011. "Skin Bleaching and Global White Supremacy: By Way of Introduction." *The Journal of Pan African Studies* 4(4):4–46.

Bleich, Erik. 2003. *Race Politics in Britain and France: Ideas and Policymaking Since the 1960s.* Cambridge, UK: Cambridge University Press.

Blight, David W. 2006. "If You Don't Tell It Like It Was, It Can Never Be as It Ought to Be." Pp. 19–34 in *Slavery and Public History: The Tough Stuff of American Memory,* edited by J. O. Horton and L. E. Horton. Chapel Hill: University of North Carolina Press.

Blumer, Herbert. 1958. "Race Prejudice as a Sense of Group Position." *Pacific Sociological Review* 1(1):3–7.

Bobo, Lawrence and Vincent L. Hutchings. 1996. "Perceptions of Racial Group Competition: Extending Blumer's Theory of Group Position to a Multiracial Social Context." *American Sociological Review* 61(6):951–72.

Bolge, Donald. 1994. *Toms, Coons, Mulattoes, Mammies, and Bucks: An Interpretive History of Blacks in American Films,* 3rd ed. New York: Continuum.

Bonilla-Silva, Eduardo. 2010. *Racism Without Racists: Color-Blind Racism and Racial Inequality in Contemporary America,* 3rd ed. Boulder, CO: Rowman and Littlefield Publishers.

Bonner, Lynn. 2020. "Hospitals Fail to Admit Some Latinos With Virus Symptoms." *The News & Observer* July 17:1A,9A.

Boskin, Joseph. 1986. *Sambo: The Rise and Demise of an American Jester*. New York: Oxford University Press.

Bouie, Jamelle. 2020. "A Twisted Conception of Liberty." *New York Times* May 10:SR9.

Branson-Potts, Hailey, Alejandra Reyes-Velarde, Matt Stiles, and Andrew J. Campa. 2020. "The Price of Being 'Essential': Latino Service Workers Bear Brunt of Coronavirus." *Los Angeles Times* May 17. Retrieved June 7, 2020 (https://www.latimes.com/california/story/2020-05-17/latino-essential-workers-coronavirus).

Buggs, Shantel Gabriel. 2017. "Does (Mixed-) Race Matter? The Role of Race in Interracial Sex, Dating, and Marriage?" *Sociology Compass* 11(11).

Cashin, Sheryll. 2017. *Loving: Interracial Intimacy in America and the Threat to White Supremacy*. Boston, MA: Beacon Press.

Charles, Nick. 2020. "For Many African Americans, the Move to 'Reopen America' Is Not a 'Black Friendly' Campaign." *NBC News* May 7. Retrieved June 7, 2020 (https://www.nbcnews.com/news/nbcblk/many-cautious-african-americans-move-reopen-america-not-black-friendly-n1200771).

Chavez-Garcia, Miroslava. 2012. *States of Delinquency: Race and Science in the Making of California's Juvenile Justice System*. Berkeley: University of California Press.

Cheung, Helier, Zhaoyin Feng, and Boer Deng. 2020. "Coronavirus: What Attacks on Asians Reveal About American Identity." *BBC News* May 27. Retrieved June 7, 2020 (https://www.bbc.com/news/world-us-canada-52714804).

Childs, Erica Chito. 2009. *Fade to Black and White: Interracial Marriages in Popular Culture*. Boulder, CO: Rowman and Littlefield.

Chou, Rosalind. 2012. *Asian American Sexual Politics*. Lanham, MD: Rowman and Littlefield.

Chou, Rosalind and Joe R. Feagin. 2008. *The Myth of the Model Minority: Asian Americans Facing Racism*. Boulder, CO: Paradigm Publishers.

Clark, Willis. 1918. "A Statistical Study of 108 Truants." *The Journal of Delinquency* 1111(5):213–34.

Coates, Ta-Nehisi. 2014. "The Case for Reparations." *The Atlantic* June. Retrieved July 15, 2020 (https://www.theatlantic.com/magazine/archive/2014/06/the-case-for-reparations/361631).

Collins, Patricia Hill. 1990. *Black Feminist Thought: Knowledge, Consciousness, and the Politics of Empowerment*. New York: Routledge.

Cooper, Hannah L. F. 2015. "War on Drugs Policing and Police Brutality." *Substance Use and Misuse* 50:1188–94.

Cornell, Stephen and Douglas Hartmann. 1998. *Ethnicity and Race: Making Identities in a Changing World*. Thousand Oaks, CA: Pine Forge Press.

"COVID-19: Fueling Anti-Asian Racism and Xenophobia Worldwide." *Human Rights Watch* May 12. Retrieved June 7, 2020 (https://www.hrw.org/news/2020/05/12/covid-19-fueling-anti-asian-racism-and-xenophobia-worldwide).

"COVID-19 in Racial and Ethnic Minority Groups." 2020. *Centers for Disease Control and Prevention* June 25. Retrieved July 17, 2020 (https://www.cdc.gov/coronavirus/2019-ncov/need-extra-precautions/racial-ethnic-minorities.html).

Cramer, Katherine. 2020. "Understanding the Role of Racism in Contemporary US Public Opinion." *Annual Review of Political Science* 23:153–69.

Crenshaw, Kimberlé. 1989. "Demarginalizing the Intersection of Race and Sex: A Black Feminist Critique of Antidiscrimination Doctrine, Feminist Theory and Antiracist Politics." *The University of Chicago Legal Forum* 140:139–67.

Cretton, Vivienne. 2018. "Performing Whiteness: Racism, Skin Colour, and Identity in Western Switzerland." *Ethnic and Racial Studies* 41(5):842–59.

Dalmage, Heather M. 2000. *Tripping on the Color Line: Black–White Multiracial Families in a Racially Divided World*. New Brunswick, NJ: Rutgers University Press.

Dalmage, Heather M. 2006. "Finding a Home: Housing the Color Line." Pp. 301–12 in *Mixed Messages: Multiracial Identities in the "Color-Blind" Era*, edited by D. L. Brunsma. Boulder, CO: Lynne Reinner Publishers.

Daly, Mary C., Bart Hobijn, and Joseph H. Pedtke. 2017. "Disappointing Facts About the Black–White Wage Gap." *FRBSF Economic Letter* Sept. 5. Retrieved June 17, 2020 (http://www.frbsf.org/economic-research/files/el2017-26.pdf).

Da Silva, Antonio José Bacelar and Erika Robb Larkins. 2019. "The Bolsonaro Election, Antiblackness, and Changing Race Relations in Brazil." *The Journal of Latin American and Caribbean Anthropology* 24(4):893–913.

Davis, Angela. 1981. *Women, Race, and Class*. New York: Vintage Books.

Davis, Angela. 2003. *Are Prisons Obsolete?* New York: Seven Stories Press.

Davis, James F. 1991. *Who Is Black? One Nation's Definition*. University Park: The Pennsylvania University Press.

Degler, Carl N. 1971. *Neither Black nor White: Slavery and Race Relations in Brazil and the United States*. Madison: University of Wisconsin Press.

Del Visco, Stephen. 2019. "Yellow Peril, Red Scare: Race and Communism in *National Review*." *Ethnic and Racial Studies* 42(4):626–44.

De Oliveira, Cleuci. 2017. "Brazil's New Problem With Blackness." *Foreign Policy* April 5. Retrieved June 16, 2020 (https://foreignpolicy.com/2017/04/05/brazils-new-problem-with-blackness-affirmative-action).

Devine, Patricia G. and Andrew J. Elliot. 1995. "Are Racial Stereotypes Really Fading? The Princeton Trilogy Revisited." *Personality and Social Psychology Bulletin* 11:1139–50.

DiAngelo, Robin. 2018. *White Fragility: Why It's So Hard for White People to Talk About Racism*. Boston, MA: Beacon Press.

Digernes, Yngve. 2020. Personal communication.

DiTomaso, Nancy. 2013. *The American Non-dilemma: Racial Inequality Without Racism*. New York: Russell Sage Foundation.

Dovidio, John F. and Samuel L. Gaertner. 2007. "Aversive Racism." *Encyclopedia of Social Psychology*, edited by R. F. Baumeister and K. D. Vohs. October. Retrieved June 27, 2020 (https://sk.sagepub.com/reference/socialpsychology/n52.xml).

Dovidio, John F., Miles Hewstone, Peter Glick, and Victoria M. Esses. 2010. "Prejudice, Stereotyping, and Discrimination: An Empirical and Theoretical Overview." Pp. 3–28 in *The SAGE Handbook of Prejudice, Stereotyping, and Discrimination*, edited by J. F. Dovidio, M. Hewstone, P. Glick, and V. M. Esses. Thousand Oaks, CA: SAGE.

Dreisinger, Baz. 2016. *Incarceration Nations*. New York: Other Press.

DuVernay, Ava. 2016. *13th*. Forward Movement Films.

Emerson, Michael O., Rachel Tolbert Kimbro, and George Yancey. 2002. "Contact Theory Extended: The Effects of Prior Racial Contact on Current Racial Ties." *Social Science Quarterly* 83(3):745–61.

Epps, Garrett. 2018. "The Citizenship Clause Means What It Says." *The Nation* October 30. Retrieved July 21, 2020 (https://www.theatlantic.com/ideas/archive/2018/10/birthright-citizenship-constitution/574381).

Escobar, Natalie. 2020. "When Xenophobia Spreads Like a Virus." *NPR* March 4. Retrieved March 13, 2020 (https://www.npr.org/2020/03/02/811363404/when-xenophobia-spreads-like-a-virus?fbclid=IwAR1S7Qjr5ZGYePdRohIARn9NwyscP6O2hdMvs81LoKNCH6pt G2Hu3MyxDXs).

Essed, Philomena and Sandra Trienekens. 2008. "'Who Wants to Feel White?' Race, Dutch Culture, and Contested Identities." *Ethnic and Racial Studies* 31(1):52–72.

Evans, Ian. 2010. *Cultures of Violence: Lynching and Racial Killing in South Africa and the American South*. Manchester, UK: Manchester University Press.

Feldman, Stanley and Leonie Huddy. 2005. "Racial Resentment and White Opposition to Race Conscious Programs: Principles or Prejudice?" *American Journal of Political Science* 49:168–83.

Feliciano, Cynthia, Belinda Robnett, and Golnaz Komaie. 2009. "Gendered Racial Exclusion Among White Internet Daters." *Social Science Research* 38(1):39–54.

Filandra, Alexandra and Noah J. Kaplan. 2016. "Racial Resentment and Whites' Gun Policy Preferences in Contemporary America." *Political Behavior* 38:255–75.

Fitzgerald, Kathleen J. 2007. *Beyond White Ethnicity: Developing a Sociological Understanding of Native American Identity Reclamation*. Lanham, MA: Lexington Books.

Fitzgerald, Kathleen J. 2014. "The Continuing Significance of Race: Racial Genomics in a Postracial Era." *Humanity and Society* 38(1):49–66.

Fitzgerald, Kathleen J. 2017a. *Recognizing Race and Ethnicity: Power, Privilege, and Inequality*, 2nd ed. New York: Routledge.

Fitzgerald, Kathleen J. 2017b. "Understanding Racialized Homophobic and Transphobic Violence." Pp. 53–70 in *Violence Against Black Bodies: An Intersectional Analysis of How Black Lives Continue to Matter*, edited by S. E. Weissinger, D. A. Mack, and E. Watson. New York: Routledge.

Fitzgerald, Kathleen J. and Kandice L. Grossman. 2017. *Sociology of Sexualities*. Thousand Oaks, CA: SAGE.

Flynn, Kerry. 2020. "Journalists of Color Are Fed Up and Speaking Out." *CNN.com* June 5. Retrieved June 20, 2020 (https://www.nytimes.com/2020/06/06/business/corporate-amer ica-has-failed-black-america.html).

Fountain, Ben. 2018. "Slavery and the Origins of the American Police State." *Medium* Sept. 17. Retrieved July 3, 2020 (https://gen.medium.com/slavery-and-the-origins-of-the-ameri can-police-state-ec318f5ff05b).

Frakt, Austin and Tony Monkovic. 2019. "A 'Rare Case Where Racial Biases' Protected African Americans." *The New York Times* Nov. 25. Retrieved June 30, 2020 (https://www .nytimes.com/2019/11/25/upshot/opioid-epidemic-blacks.html).

Frankenberg, Ruth. 1993. *The Social Construction of Whiteness: White Women, Race Matters.* Minneapolis: University of Minnesota Press.

Freyre, Gilberto. 1933. *The Masters and Slaves: A Study in the Development of Brazilian Civilization.* Berkeley: University of California Press.

Gaddis, S. Michael. 2019. "Understanding the 'How' and 'Why' Aspects of Racial-Ethnic Discrimination: A Multimethod Approach to Audit Studies." *Sociology of Race and Ethnicity* 5(4):443–55.

Gaertner, Samuel L. and John F. Dovidio. 1986. "The Aversive Form of Racism." Pp. 61–89 in *Prejudice, Discrimination, and Racism*, edited by S. L. Gaertner and J. F. Dovidio. Orlando, FL: Academic Press.

Gans, Herbert J. 1996 [1979]. "Symbolic Ethnicity: The Future of Ethnic Groups and Cultures in America." Pp. 425–59 in *Theories of Ethnicity: A Classical Reader*, edited by W. Sollors. New York: New York University Press.

Gelles, David. 2020. "Corporate America Has Failed Black America." *New York Times* June 7. Retrieved June 20, 2020 (https://www.nytimes.com/2020/06/06/business/corporate-amer ica-has-failed-black-america.html).

Gilroy, Paul. 1993. *The Black Atlantic: Modernity and Double-Consciousness.* Cambridge, MA: Harvard University Press.

Gittleman, Maury and Edward N. Wolff. 2004. "Racial Differences in Patterns of Wealth Accumulation." *The Journal of Human Resources* 39(1):193–227.

Glazer, Nathan and Daniel Patrick Moynihan. 1963. *Beyond the Melting Pot.* Cambridge, MA: MIT Press.

Godoy, Maria and Daniel Wood. 2020. "What Do Coronavirus Racial Disparities Look Like State by State?" *NPR* May 30. Retrieved June 3, 2020 (https://www.npr.org/sections/health-shots/2020/05/30/865413079/what-do-coronavirus-racial-disparities-look-like-state-by-state).

Goings, Kenneth W. 1994. *Mammy and Uncle Mose: Black Collectibles and American Stereotyping.* Bloomington: Indiana University Press.

Golash-Boza, Tanya. 2011. *Yo Soy Negro: Blackness in Peru.* Gainesville: University of Florida Press.

Goldberg, David Theo. 2006. "Racial Europeanization." *Ethnic and Racial Studies* 29:331–64.

Goo, Sara Kehaulani. 2015. "How Pew Research Center Conducted Its Survey of Multiracial Americans." *Pew Research Center* June 11. Retrieved July 9, 2020 (https://www.pewresearch.org/fact-tank/2015/06/11/how-pew-research-conducted-its-survey-of-multiracial-americans).

Gordon, Milton. 1964. *Assimilation in American Life*. New York: Oxford University Press.

Green, Victor H. 1949. *Negro Motorist Green Book*. New York: Victor H. Green, Publisher.

Grzanka, Patrick R. 2014. *Intersectionality: A Foundations and Frontiers Reader*. Boulder, CO: Westview Press.

Gullickson, Aaron and Florencia Torche. 2014. "Patterns of Racial and Educational Assortative Mating in Brazil." *Demography* 51:835–36.

Hansen, Marcus Lee. 1996 [1938]. "The Problem of the Third Generation Immigrant." Pp. 202–15 in *Theories of Ethnicity: A Classical Reader*, edited by W. Sollors. New York: New York University Press.

Harris, Elizabeth A. 2020. "People Are Marching Against Racism. They're Also Reading About It." *The New York Times* June 5. Retrieved July 18, 2020 (https://www.nytimes.com/2020/06/05/books/antiracism-books-race-racism.html).

Harris, Melvin. 1964. *Patterns of Race in the Americas*. New York: W.W. Norton.

Hartlep, Nicholas Daniel. 2013. *The Model Minority Stereotype: Demystifying Asian American Success*. Charlotte, NC: Information Age Publishing.

Hatch, John B. 2016. "'Accidental Racist': Stumbling Through the Motions of Racial Reconciliation." *Communication Quarterly* 64(1):93–118.

Heerwig, Jennifer A. and Brian J. McCabe. 2009. "Education and Social Desirability Bias: The Case of a Black Presidential Candidate." *Social Science Quarterly* 90(3):674–86.

Hello, Evelyn, Peer Scheepers, and Mérove Gijsberts. 2002. "Educations and Ethnic Prejudice in Europe: Explanations for Cross-National Variances in the Educational Effect on Ethnic Prejudice." *Scandinavian Journal of Educational Research* 46(1):5–24.

Hello, Evelyn, Peer Scheepers, and Peter Sleegers. 2006. "Why the More Educated Are Less Inclined to Keep Ethnic Distance: An Empirical Test of Four Explanations." *Ethnic and Racial Studies* 29(5):959–85.

Herring, Cedric, Verna M. Keith, and Hayward Derrick Horton, eds. 2003. *Skin Deep: How Race and Complexion Matter in the "Color Blind" Era*. Chicago: Institute for Research on Race and Public Policy, University of Illinois at Chicago.

Hirschfelder, Arlene and Paulette F. Molin. 2019. "Stereotyping Native Americans." *Jim Crow Museum of Racist Memorabilia at Ferris State University*. Retrieved July 3, 2020 (https://www.ferris.edu/HTMLS/news/jimcrow/native/homepage.htm).

Hirschman Dan. 2020. "Levels of Racism: Individual, Organizational, Institutional, and Systemic." *Scatterplot: The Unruly Darlings of Public Sociology* June 22. Retrieved June 24, 2020 (https://scatter.wordpress.com).

Hochschild, Jennifer, Vesla Weaver, and Traci Burch. 2012. *Creating a New Racial Order: How Immigration, Multiracialism, Genomics, and the Young Can Remake Race in America*. Princeton, NJ: Princeton University Press.

"Household Income: 2018." 2019. *American Community Survey Briefs* September. Retrieved June 17, 2020 (https://www.census.gov/content/dam/Census/library/publications/2019/acs/acsbr18-01.pdf).

Howell, Junia, Marie Skoczylan, and Shataé DeVaughn. 2019. "Living While Black." *Contexts* 18(2):68–69.

Hummer, Robert. 2020. "The COVID-19 Health Toll in the United States: Exposing Racism . . . Yet Again." *The Department of Sociology* May 22. Retrieved May 23, 2020 (https://sociology.unc.edu/the-covid-19-health-toll-in-the-united-states-exposing-racism-yet-again).

Hunter, Margaret. 2005. *Race, Gender, and the Politics of Skin Tone.* New York: Routledge.

Hurwitz, Jon, Mark Peffley, and Paul Sniderman. 1997. "Racial Stereotypes and Whites' Political Views of Blacks in the Context of Welfare and Crime." *American Journal of Political Science* 41:30–60.

Jan, Tracy. 2020. "This Is How Economic Pain Is Distributed in America." *The Washington Post* May 9. Retrieved June 1, 2020 (https://www.washingtonpost.com/business/2020/05/09/jobs-report-demographics).

Jones, Gavin W. 2003. "White Australia, National Identity, and Population Change." Pp. 110–28 in *Legacies of White Australia: Race, Culture, and Nation*, edited by L. Jayasuriya, D. Walker, and J. Gothard. Crawley, Western Australia: University of Western Australia Press.

Jones, Martha S. 2018. *Birthright Citizens: A History of Race and Rights in Antebellum America.* Cambridge, UK: Cambridge University Press.

Jordan, Winthrop. 1968. *White Over Black: American Attitudes Toward the Negro, 1550–1812.* Chapel Hill: University of North Carolina Press.

Joyner, Kara and Grace Kao. 2005. "Interracial Relationships and the Transition to Adulthood." *American Sociological Review* 70(4):563–81.

"Justice Compromised: The Legacy of Rwanda's Community-Based Gacaca Courts." 2011. *Human Rights Watch* May 31. Retrieved July 21, 2020 (https://www.hrw.org/report/2011/05/31/justice-compromised/legacy-rwandas-community-based-gacaca-courts#).

Kacere, Laura. 2014. "Transmisogyny 101: What It Is and What Can We Do About It?" *Everyday Feminism* Jan. 27. Retrieved Feb. 1, 2018 (https://everydayfeminism.com/2014/01/transmisogyny).

Kallberg, Arnie L. 2020. "COVID-19, Precarity, and Worker Power." *Department of Sociology* May 22. Retrieved May 23, 2020 (https://sociology.unc.edu/covid-19-precarity-and-worker-power).

Kapitan, Alex. 2019. "Re-humanizing Immigrant Communities in the Age of Trump: 5 Language Practices." *Radical Copy Editor* July 22. Retrieved July 21, 2020 (https://radicalcopyeditor.com/2019/07/22/re-humanizing-immigrant-communities).

Katznelson, Ira. 2005. *When Affirmative Action Was White: An Untold Story of Racial Inequality in Twentieth-Century America.* New York: W.W. Norton and Company.

Kawai, Yuko. 2005. "Stereotyping Asian Americans: The Dialect of the Model Minority and the Yellow Peril." *Howard Journal of Communications* 16(2):109–30.

Kendi, Ibram X. 2019a. *How to Be an Antiracist.* New York: OneWorld.

Kendi, Ibram X. 2019b. "The Greatest White Privilege Is Life Itself." *The Atlantic* Oct. 24. Retrieved Feb. 16, 2020 (https://www.theatlantic.com/ideas/archive/2019/10/too-short-lives-black-men/600628/?utm_content=edit-promo&utm_term=2019-10-24T15%3A49%3A29&utm_medium=social&utm_campaign=the-atlantic&utm_source=facebook&fbclid=IwAR3db89v5tTF85jll2pXFuZ5m1Tik_oJnA9c7pcHL-mDQDMU3Q70DBj_1z0).

Kennedy, Randall. 2003. *Interracial Intimacies: Sex, Marriage, Identity, and Adoption.* New York: Vintage Books Edition.

Khanna, Nikki. 2020. *Whiter: Asian American Women on Skin Color and Colorism.* New York: New York University Press.

Kinder, Donald and Lynn Sanders. 1996. *Divided by Color: Racial Politics and Democratic Ideals.* Chicago, IL: University of Chicago Press.

Knaus, Christopher B. and M. Christopher Brown II. 2016. *Whiteness in the New South Africa: Qualitative Research on Post-Apartheid Racism.* New York: Peter Lang Publishers.

Knuckey, Jonathan and Myunghee Kim. 2016. "Racial Resentment, Old-Fashioned Racism, and the Vote Choice of Southern and Nonsouthern Whites in the 2012 US Presidential Election." *Social Science Quarterly* 96(4):905–22.

Korgen, Kathleen Odell. 1998. *From Black to Biracial: Transforming Racial Identity Among Americans.* Westport, CT: Praeger Publishers.

"Labor Force Characteristics by Race and Ethnicity, 2018." 2019. *Bureau of Labor Statistics* October. Retrieved July 22, 2020 (https://www.bls.gov/opub/reports/race-and-ethnicity/2018/home.htm#:~:text=The%20employment%E2%80%93population%20ratio%20was,%2C%205%2C%20and%205A).

Lake, Marilyn and Henry Reynolds. 2008. *Drawing the Global Colour Line: White Men's Countries and the International Challenges of Racial Equality.* Cambridge, UK: Cambridge University Press.

Lakhani, Nina. 2020. "US Coronavirus Hotspots Linked to Meat Processing Plants." *The Guardian* May 15. Retrieved June 7, 2020 (https://www.theguardian.com/world/2020/may/15/us-coronavirus-meat-packing-plants-food).

Laszloffy, Tracey and Kerry Ann Rockquemore. 2013. "What About the Children? Exploring Misconceptions and Realities About Mixed-Race Children." Pp. 45–66 in *Interracial Relationships in the 21st Century*, 2nd ed., edited by E. Smith and A. J. Hattery. Durham, NC: Carolina Academic Press.

Leal, David L. 2003. "The Multicultural Military: Military Service and the Acculturation of Latinos and Anglos." *Armed Forces and Society* 29(2):205–26.

Lee, Matthew. 2020. "Coronavirus Fears Show How 'Model Minority' Asian Americans Become the 'Yellow Peril.'" *NBC News.com* March 9. Retrieved March 11, 2020 (https://www.nbcnews.com/think/opinion/coronavirus-fears-show-how-model-minority-asian-americans-become-yellow-ncna1151671?fbclid=IwAR0qTq1noQRGyrQjRMU0bIQB920m2QpNNCqE7DS6GDhRFGL2DiDrEaqB-V4).

Lee, Robert G. 1999. *Orientals: Asian Americans in Popular Culture*. Philadelphia, PA: Temple University Press.

Less, Stacey J. 2009. *Unraveling the "Model Minority" Stereotype: Listening to Asian American Youth*, 2nd ed. New York: Teachers College Press.

"Lesson 1: What Is Restorative Justice?" n.d. *Centre for Justice and Reconciliation*. Retrieved March 13, 2020 (http://restorativejustice.org/restorative-justice/about-restorative-justice/tutorial-intro-to-restorative-justice/lesson-1-what-is-restorative-justice/#sthash.MqNPo5Yl .dpbs).

Lew, Jamie. 2003. *Asian Americans in Class: Charting the Achievement Gap Among Korean American Youth*. New York: Teachers College Press.

Lienemann, Brianna A. and Heather T. Stopp. 2013. "The Association Between Media Exposure of Interracial Relationships and Attitudes Toward Interracial Relationships." *Journal of Applied Social Psychology* 43(S2):E398–E415.

Lin, Ken-Hou and Jennifer H. Lundquist. 2013. "Mate Selection in Cyberspace: The Intersection of Race, Gender, and Education." *American Journal of Sociology* 119(1):183–215.

Livingston, Gretchen and Anna Brown. 2017. "Trends and Patterns in Intermarriage." *Pew Research Center* May 18. Retrieved July 12, 2020 (https://www.pewsocialtrends .org/2017/05/18/1-trends-and-patterns-in-intermarriage).

Lopez, Mark Huge, Lee Rainie, and Abby Budiman. 2020. "Financial and Health Impacts of COVID-19 Vary Widely by Race and Ethnicity." *Pew Research Center* May 5. Retrieved May 21, 2020 (https://www.pewresearch.org/fact-tank/2020/05/05/financial-and-health-impacts-of-covid-19-vary-widely-by-race-and-ethnicity).

Lundquist, Jennifer H. and Ken-Hou Lin. 2015. "Is Love (Color) Blind? The Economy of Race Among Gay and Straight Daters." *Social Forces* 93(4):1423–49.

Madon, Stephanie, Max Guyll, Kathy Aboufadel, Eulices Montiel, Alison Smith, Polly Palumbro, and Lee Jussim. 2001. "Ethnic and National Stereotypes: The Princeton Trilogy Revisited and Revised." *Personality and Social Psychology Bulletin* 27:996–1010.

Magee, Rhonda V. 2019. *The Inner Work of Racial Justice: Healing Ourselves and Transforming Our Communities Through Mindfulness*. New York: Tarcher Perigee.

Mallett, Kandist. 2020. "'Reopen Protests' Are Motivated by Racism, Lack of Concern for Black and Brown Lives." *Teen Vogue* May 1. Retrieved June 7, 2020 (https://www.nbcnews .com/news/nbcblk/many-cautious-african-americans-move-reopen-america-not-black-friendly-n1200771).

Mangum, Maruice and LaTasha DeHaan. 2019. "Entitlement and Perceived Racial Discrimination: The Missing Links to White Opinions on Affirmative Action and Preferential Hiring and Promotion." *American Politics Research* 47(2):415–42.

Massey, Douglas and Nancy Denton. 1993. *American Apartheid: Segregation and the Making of the Underclass*. Cambridge, MA: Harvard University Press.

McClintock, Anne. 1995. *Imperial Leather: Race, Gender, Sexuality and the Colonial Contest*. New York: Routledge.

McLaurin, Virginia. 2019. "Why the Myth of the Savage Indian Persists." *Sapiens.org* Feb. 27. Retrieved July 3, 2020 (https://www.sapiens.org/culture/native-american-stereotypes).

McLemore, S. Dale and Harriet D. Romo. 2005. *Racial and Ethnic Relations in America*, 7th ed. New York: Pearson.

Meeusen, Cecil, Thomas de Vroome, and Mark Hooghe. 2013. "How Does Education Have an Impact on Ethnocentrism? A Structural Equation Analysis of Cognitive, Occupational Status and Network Mechanisms." *International Journal of Intercultural Relations* 3(7):507–22.

Menchik, Paul L. and Nancy Ammon Jiankoplos. 1997. "Black–White Wealth Inequality: Is Inheritance the Reason?" *Economic Inquiry* 35(2):428–42.

Merton, Robert. 1976. "Discrimination and the American Creed." Pp. 1999–2016 in *Sociological Ambivalence and Other Essays*. New York: Free Press.

Metzl, Jonathan M. 2019. *Dying of Whiteness: How the Politics of Racial Resentment Is Killing America's Heartland*. New York: Basic Books.

Mineo, Liz. 2020. "For Native Americans, COVID-19 Is the 'Worst of Both Worlds at the Same Time.'" *The Harvard Gazette* May 8. Retrieved May 21, 2020 (https://news.harvard.edu/gazette/story/2020/05/the-impact-of-covid-19-on-native-american-communities).

Mitchell, Megan and Mark Wells. 2018. "Race, Romantic Attraction, and Dating." *Ethical Theory and Moral Practice* 21:945–61.

Moore, Lisa D. and Amy Elkavich. 2008. "Who's Using and Who's Doing Time? Incarceration, the War on Drugs, and Public Health." *American Journal of Public Health* 98(5):782–86.

Moore, Tina. 2020. "Asian Man Is Victim in Latest Coronavirus-Fueled Hate Crime." *New York Post* March 11. Retrieved March 13, 2020 (https://nypost.com/2020/03/11/asian-man-is-victim-in-latest-coronavirus-fueled-hate-crime/?fbclid=IwAR3M_uE_uPU7D8Q8sMcqbiZ1hD7q8crps8mjyc5bwzz15kpHCjxH_VQ45ug).

Moore, Wendy. 2008. *Reproducing Racism: White Space, Elite Law Schools, and Racial Inequality*. Lanham, MD: Rowman and Littlefield.

Morris, Aldon D. 2015. *The Scholar Denied: W.E.B. DuBois and the Birth of Modern Sociology*. Oakland: University of California Press.

Moskos, Charles C. and John Sibley Butler. 1996. *All That We Can Be: Black Leadership and Racial Integration the Army Way*. New York: Basic Books.

Muhammad, Dedrick Asante, Rogelio Tec, and Kathy Ramirez. 2019. "Racial Wealth Snapshot: American Indians/Native Americans." *NCRC National Community Reinvestment Coalition* November 18. Retrieved June 17, 2020 (https://ncrc.org/racial-wealth-snapshot-american-indians-native-americans).

Nagel, Joane. 1996. *American Indian Ethnic Renewal: Red Power and the Resurgence of Identity and Culture*. Oxford, UK: Oxford University Press.

Nelson, Alondra. 2016. *The Social Life of DNA*. New York: Penguin/Random House.

Nguyen, Jenny, Shannon K. Carter, and J. Scott Carter. 2019. "From Yellow Peril to Model Minority: Perceived Threat by Asian Americans in Employment." *Social Science Quarterly* 100(3):565–77.

Noah, Trevor. 2016. *Born a Crime*. New York: Spiegel and Grau/Random House.

Nunn, Kenneth B. 2002. "Race, Crime, and the Surplus Pool of Criminality: Or Why the 'War on Drugs' Was a 'War on Blacks.'" *Journal of Gender, Race, and Justice* 6:381–445.

Okihiro, Gary Y. 1994. *Margins and Mainstreams: Asians in American History and Culture.* Seattle: University of Washington.

Oliver, Melvin L. and Thomas M. Shapiro. 1995. *Black Wealth/White Wealth: A New Perspective on Racial Inequality.* New York: Routledge.

Oliver, Melvin and Thomas M. Shapiro. 2019. "Disrupting the Racial Wealth Gap." *Contexts* Winter:16–21. Retrieved June 3, 2020 (https://journals.sagepub.com/doi/pdf/10.1177/1536504219830672).

Omi, Michael and Howard Winant. 1994. *Racial Formations in the United States: From the 1960s to the 1990s*, 2nd ed. New York: Routledge.

Onwuachi-Willig, Angela. 2013. *According to Our Hearts:* Rhinelander v. Rhinelander *and the Law of the Multiracial Family.* New Haven, CT: Yale University Press.

Osuji, Chinyere. 2013. "Confronting Whitening in an Era of Black Consciousness: Racial Ideology and Black–White Interracial Marriages in Rio de Janeiro." *Ethnic and Racial Studies* 36(10):1490–1506.

Pager, Devah. 2003. "The Mark of a Criminal Record." *The American Journal of Sociology* 108(5):937–75.

Paolini, Stefania, Miles Hewstone, and Ed Cairns. 2007. "Direct and Indirect Intergroup Friendship Effects: Testing the Moderating Role of the Affective-Cognitive Bases of Prejudice." *Personality and Social Psychology Bulletin* 33:1406–20.

Park, Robert Ezra. 1950. *Race and Culture.* Glencoe, IL: The Free Press.

Pearson, Adam R., John F. Dovidio, and Samuel L. Gaertner. 2009. "The Nature of Contemporary Prejudice: Insights From Aversive Racism." *Social and Personality Psychology Compass* 3(3):314–38.

Persons, Stow. 1987. *Ethnic Studies at Chicago: 1905–1945.* Champaign: University of Illinois Press.

Pettigrew, Thomas F. and Linda R.Tropp. 2006. "A Meta-Analytic Test of Intergroup Contact Theory." *Journal of Personality and Social Psychology* 90:751–83.

Pinho, Patricia de Santana. 2009. "White, but Not Quite: Tones and Overtones of Whiteness in Brazil." *Small Axe* 13(2):39–56.

Portes, Alejandro and Min Zhou. 1993. "The New Second Generation: Segmented Assimilation and It's Variants Among Post-1965 Immigrant Youth." *The Annals of the American Academy of Political and Social Sciences* 530:74–96.

Portes, Alejandro and Rubén G. Rumbaut. 2001. *Legacies: The Story of the Immigrant Second Generation.* Berkeley: University of California Press.

Powell, J. and Eileen B. Hershenov. 1990. "Hostage to the Drug War: The National Purse, the Constitution, and the Black Community." *University of California Davis Law Review* 24:557–616.

Pygas, Mark. 2020. "Republicans Are Calling COVID-19 'Chinese Coronavirus' Despite Racist Attacks Against Asians." *Upworthy* March 10. Retrieved March 11, 2020 (https://megaphone.upworthy.com/p/republicans-chinese-coronavirus?fbclid=IwAR29p2jV4S1j9lQyXyjohd9VKnwAs3RrBRSOaYlMVtCmtGydmixMzPhw2hU).

Quadagno, Jill. 1994. *The Color of Welfare.* Oxford, UK: Oxford University Press.

Quillian, Lincoln, Devah Pager, Ole Hexel, and Arnfin H. Midtbøen. 2017. "Meta-Analysis of Field Experiments Shows No Change in Racial Discrimination Hiring Over Time." *PNAS: Proceedings of the National Academy of the Sciences of the United States of America* 114(41):10870–5.

Ray, Rashawn. 2020. "What Does 'Defund Police' Mean and Does It Have Merit?" *Brookings Institute* June 19. Retrieved July 19, 2020 (https://www.brookings.edu/blog/fixgov/2020/06/19/what-does-defund-the-police-mean-and-does-it-have-merit).

Ray, Victor. 2020. "Antiracism Is a Constant Struggle." *Contexts* Spring 19(3):74–76.

Reeves, Jay. 2020. "In Clamor to Reopen, Many African Americans Feel Their Safety Is Being Ignored." *PBS.org* May 5. Retrieved June 7, 2020 (https://www.pbs.org/newshour/economy/in-clamor-to-reopen-many-african-americans-feel-their-safety-is-ignored).

Rhea, Joseph Tilda. 1997. *Race Pride and the American Identity.* Cambridge, MA: Harvard University Press.

Ringer, Benjamin B. and Elinor R. Lawless. 1989. *Race-Ethnicity and Society.* London, UK: Routledge.

Robnett, Belinda and Cynthia Feliciano. 2011. "Patterns of Racial-Ethnic Exclusion by Internet Daters." *Social Forces* 89(3):807–28.

Rockquemore, Kerry Ann and David L. Brunsma. 2002. *Beyond Black: Biracial Identity in America.* Thousand Oaks, CA: SAGE.

Romano, Renee C. 2003. *Race Mixing: Black–White Marriage in Post-War America.* Cambridge, MA: Harvard University Press.

Ross, Jenna. 2020. "The Racial Wealth Gap in America: Asset Types Held by Race." *Visual Capitalist* June 12. Retrieved June 17, 2020 (https://www.visualcapitalist.com/racial-wealth-gap).

Rothenberg, Paula. 2015. *White Privilege: Essential Readings on the Other Side of Racism,* 5th ed. New York: Worth Publishers.

Rothstein, Richard. 2017. *The Color of Law: A Forgotten History of How Our Government Segregated America.* New York: Liveright Publishing Corporation.

Rudder, Christian. 2014. *Dataclysm: Who We Are (When We Think No One's Looking).* New York: Crown Publishers.

Sáenz, Rogelio and Karen Manges Douglas. 2015. "A Call for the Racialization of Immigration Studies: On the Transition From Ethnic Immigrants to Racial Immigrants." *Sociology of Race and Ethnicity* 1(1):161–80.

Sammut, Gordon and George Gaskell. 2010. "Points of View, Social Positioning and Intercultural Relations." *Journal for the Theory of Social Behaviour* 40(10):47–64.

Schuman, Howard, Charlotte Steeh, Lawrence D. Bobo, and Maria Kryson. 1997. *Racial Attitudes in America: Trends and Interpretations.* Cambridge, MA: Harvard University Press.

Selod, Saher. 2018. *Forever Suspect: Racialized Surveillance of Muslim Americans in the War on Terror.* New Brunswick, NJ: Rutgers University Press.

Shaheen, Jack G. 2014. *Reel Bad Arabs*, 3rd ed. Northampton, MA: Olive Branch.

Shihipar, Abdullah. 2019. "The Opioid Crisis Isn't White." *The New York Times* Feb. 26. Retrieved July 3, 2020 (https://www.nytimes.com/2019/02/26/opinion/opioid-crisis-drug-users.html).

Silverman, Hollie, Konstantin Toropin, and Sara Sidner. 2020. "Navaho Nation Surpasses New York State for the Highest COVID-19 Infection Rate in the US." *CNN.com* May 18. Retrieved June 4, 2020 (https://www.cnn.com/2020/05/18/us/navajo-nation-infection-rate-trnd/index.html).

Skrentny, John. 2014. *After Civil Rights: Racial Realism in the American Workplace*. Princeton, NJ: Princeton University Press.

Smith, Stacey L., Marc Choueiti, Ariana Case, Katherine Pieper, Hannah Clark, Karla Hernandez, Jacqueline Martinez, Benjamin Lopez, and Mauricio Mota. 2019. "Latinos in Film: Erasure on Screen and Behind the Camera Across 1,200 Popular Movies." *USC Annenberg Inclusion Initiative* August. Retrieved July 3, 2020 (http://assets.uscannenberg.org/docs/aii-study-latinos-in-film-2019.pdf).

Sollors, Werner, ed. 1996. *Theories of Ethnicity: A Classical Reader.* New York: New York University Press.

Sollors, Werner. 2017. *Challenges of Diversity: Essays on America.* New Brunswick, NJ: Rutgers University Press.

Soutphommasane, Tim. 2019. "The Cultural Power of Whiteness in Australia." *Sun Herald* Feb. 10. Retrieved June 11, 2020 (https://search-proquest-com.libproxy.lib.unc.edu/docview/2177630792?pq-origsite=summon).

Spickard, Paul. 1989. *Mixed Blood: Intermarriage and Ethnic Identity in Twentieth Century America.* Madison: University of Wisconsin Press.

Stainback, Kevin and Donald Tomaskovic-Devey. 2012. *Documenting Desegregation: Racial and Gender Segregation in Private Sector Employment Since the Civil Rights Act.* New York: Russell Sage Foundation.

Stein, Howard and Robert F. Hill. 1977. *The Ethnic Imperative: Examining the New White Ethnic Movement.* University Park: Pennsylvania University Press.

Steinbugler, Amy C. 2012. *Beyond Loving: Intimate Racework in Lesbian, Gay, and Straight Interracial Relationships.* New York: Oxford University Press.

Stevens, Garth. 2014. "Racialization and Deracialization." *Encyclopedia of Critical Psychology*, edited by T. Teo. Retrieved July 21, 2020 (https://link.springer.com/referenceworkentry/10.1007%2F978-1-4614-5583-7_258).

Stolberg, Sheryl Gay. 2019. "At Historic Hearing, House Panel Explores Reparations." *The New York Times* June 19. Retrieved July 19, 2020 (https://www.nytimes.com/2019/06/19/us/politics/slavery-reparations-hearing.html).

Stumpf, Juliet P. 2006. "The Crimmigration Crisis: Immigrants, Crime, and Sovereign Power." *American University Law Review* 56(2):367–419.

Sue, Christina A. 2013. *Land of the Cosmic Race: Race Mixture, Racism, and Blackness in Mexico.* New York: Oxford University Press.

Sullivan, Kate. 2019. "I Honestly Don't See Color." *CNN Politics* Feb. 13. Retrieved Feb. 14, 2019 (https://www.cnn.com/2019/02/13/politics/howard-schultz-see-color/index.html).

Suneson, Grant and Samuel Stebbins. 2019. "These 15 Countries Have the Widest Gaps Between Rich and the Poor." *USA Today* May 28. Retrieved June 14, 2020 (https://www.usatoday.com/story/money/2019/05/28/countries-with-the-widest-gaps-between-rich-and-poor/39510157).

Takaki, Ronald. 1990. *Iron Cages: Race and Culture in 19th Century America.* New York: Oxford University Press.

Takaki, Ronald. 1993. *A Different Mirror: A History of Multicultural America.* Boston, MA: Little, Brown and Company.

Tam, Tania, Miles Hewstone, Jared B.Kenworthy, Ed Cairns, Claudia Marinetti, Leo Geddes, et al. 2008. "Postconflict Reconciliation: Intergroup Forgiveness and Implicit Biases in Northern Ireland." *Journal of Social Issues* 64:303–20.

Taylor, Candacy. 2020. *Overground Railroad: The Green Book and the Roots of Black Travel in America.* New York: Abrams Press.

Telles, Edward. 2004. *Race in Another America: The Significance of Skin Color in Brazil.* Princeton, NJ: Princeton University Press

Telles, Edward and the Project on Ethnicity and Race in Latin America. 2014. *Pigmentocracies: Ethnicity, Race, and Color in Latin America.* Chapel Hill: University of North Carolina Press.

Teranishi, Robert T. 2010. *Asians in the Ivory Tower: Dilemmas of Racial Inequality in American Higher Education.* New York: Teachers College Press.

Terrell, Henry S. 1971. "Wealth Accumulation of Black and White Families: The Empirical Evidence." *Journal of Finance* 26(2):363–77.

"The Population of Poverty USA." 2019. *Poverty Facts: PovertyUSA.org.* Retrieved June 19, 2020 (https://www.povertyusa.org/facts).

"The Problem . . ." 2020. *Campaign Zero.* Retrieved July 18, 2020 (https://www.joincampaign zero.org/problem).

Thomas, William I. and Florian Znaniecki. 1918–1920. *The Polish Peasant in Europe and America: Monograph of an Immigrant Group.* Boston, MA: Richard G. Badger.

Tipton-Martin, Toni. 2020. "Freedom Is a Gift: How the Women of the Jemima Code Freed Me." *The New York Times* June 21:ST7.

Tonry, Michael. 1994a. "Race and the War on Drugs." *The University of Chicago Legal Forum* 25:25–81.

Tonry, Michael. 1994b. "Racial Politics, Racial Disparities, and the War on Crime." *Crime and Delinquency* 40(4):475–94.

Tsunokai, Glenn T, Allison R. McGrath, and Jillian K. Kavanagh. 2014. "Online Dating Preferences of Asian Americans." *Journal of Social and Personal Relationships* 31(6):796–814.

Van Cleve, Nicole Gonzalez. 2016. *Crook County: Racism and Injustice in America's Largest Criminal Court.* Stanford, CA: Stanford Law Books.

Vinson, Liz. 2020. "Family Separation Policy Continues Two Years After Trump Administration Claims It Ended." *Southern Poverty Law Center* June 18. Retrieved July 20, 2020 (https://www.splcenter.org/news/2020/06/18/family-separation-policy-continues-two-years-after-trump-administration-claims-it-ended).

Wade, Peter. 2017. *Degrees of Mixture, Degrees of Freedom: Genomics, Multiculturalism, and Race in Latin America.* Durham, NC: Duke University Press.

Wagner, Ulrich and Andreas Zick. 1995. "The Relation of Formal Education to Ethnic Prejudice: Its Reliability, Validity, and Explanation." *European Journal of Social Psychology* 25:41–56.

Walker, Alice. 1983. "If the Present Looks Like the Past, What Does the Future Look Like?" In *In Search of Our Mothers' Gardens.* San Diego, CA: Harvest Books.

Ward, Marguerite. 2020. "*The New York Times* Bestseller List This Week Is Almost Entirely Composed of Books About Race and White Privilege in America." *Business Insider* June 11. Retrieved July 18, 2020 (https://www.businessinsider.com/new-york-times-bestseller-list-books-about-race-in-america-2020-6).

Waters, Mary. 1990. *Ethnic Options: Choosing Identities in America.* Berkeley: University of California Press.

Weinberg, Meyer. 1997. *Asian American Education: Historical Background and Current Realities.* Mahwah, NJ: Erlbaum Associates Publishers.

Weiner, Melissa. 2012. "Towards a Critical Global Race Theory." *Sociological Compass* 6(4):332–50.

Wetts, Rachel and Rob Willer. 2018. "Privilege on the Precipice: Perceived Racial Status Threats Lead White Americans to Oppose Welfare Programs." *Social Forces* 97(2):793–822.

Williams, Kim. 2006. *Mark One or More: Civil Rights in Multiracial America.* Ann Arbor: University of Michigan Press.

Williams, Linda Faye. 2003. *The Constraint of Race: The Legacies of White Skin Privilege in America.* University Park: Pennsylvania State University Press.

Wilson, William Julius. 1996. *When Work Disappears: The World of the New Urban Poor.* New York: Alfred A. Knopf.

Winant, Howard. 2015. "The Dark Matter of Race: Race and Racism in the 21st Century." *Critical Sociology* 41(2):313–24.

Wright, Michelle M. 2004. *Becoming Black: Creating Identity in the African Diaspora.* Durham, NC: Duke University Press.

Worden, Nigel. 2007. *The Making of Modern South Africa: Conquest, Apartheid, and Democracy.* Malden, MA: Wiley-Blackwell.

Yancey, George. 2002. "Who Interracially Dates? An Examination of the Characteristics of Those Who Have Interracially Dated." *Journal of Comparative Family Studies* 33(2):179–90.

Yancey, George and Richard Lewis, Jr. 2009. *Interracial Families: Current Concepts and Controversies.* New York: Routledge.

Index

Made in the USA
Monee, IL
11 January 2022